Dedication

For my wonderful wife Judy and son Jacques, and my family, whose support over many years has enabled me to live my dream. Also many thanks to all the Academy members and instructors, past and present, for their support and for helping me to refine my knowledge.

Bob Breen

fighting

A path to understanding

✳ snowbooks

The advice and techniques in this book should only be undertaken by martial arts students in a dojo environment who are supervised by a qualified teacher and who hold specialist martial artist insurance. Whilst every effort has been made to ensure that the content of this book is technically accurate and as sound as possible, neither the author nor the publishers can accept responsibility for any damage, injury or loss sustained as a result of the use of this material.

© Bob Breen 2006

Photography by Pete Drinkell

Edited by Emma Barnes

Designed by Emma Barnes and Stephanie de Howes

First edition

Proudly published in 2006 by

Snowbooks Ltd

120 Pentonville Road

London

N1 9JN

0207 837 6482

www.snowbooks.com

Feedback? Ideas? Let us know at info@snowbooks.com

1-905005-07-5

978-1905005-07-9

Contents

Introduction

Introduction

Principles

I have had a life-long interest in understanding fighting and martial arts and from an early age had wanted to learn the principles that underlie combat, both physical and mental. In my forty years of martial arts training it has been Jeet Kune Do, the fighting system developed by the late Bruce Lee, which has stood out amongst all the martial arts that I've studied. Jeet Kune Do is a principles-based system that has enabled me to see all my other, more traditional, training in context and to have a deeper and clearer comprehension of it. It has shortened the time I've needed to become functional in whichever type of combat I've chosen. The cross-training approach of JKD, and its emphasis on flow and adaptability, means that in a street self-defence situation it's easy to come up with instant responses to immediate dangers. In this book I've used a principles-based approach using concepts familiar to all martial arts, because from one principle a thousand techniques flow.

The aim of this book

I have written this book to give beginners and intermediate students a guide to learning and training martial arts that isn't limited to the techniques being taught; it also gives an idea of how the whole thing works. When I sat down to write it, I set out to help students along the way by providing an understanding of how principles and other tenets could inform and improve the learning and training process. I wanted to show not only what techniques to use but, more importantly, why, when and how to use them. This was the book that I needed when I was learning how to fight. A secondary aim was to write a book that the advanced student could dip into occasionally.

At the early stage of my martial arts study I bought books by Oyama and Nakayama on Karate. These were great books but didn't quite fit the style of fighting I was doing or answer the sorts of questions that I had. However, the completeness of these books has never left me and I have sought to emulate that here, as well as to provide a source-book to satisfy students' questions.

It would have been easy to write a book that impressed my peers or that showed lots of fancy techniques that didn't fit together in a logical order. Teaching on a nightly basis and doing seminars around the world has shown me people's training needs, and thus where the focus of this book should be. This book is simply about learning how to fight in a modern and functional fashion. It hasn't been my intention to cover the techniques developed by Bruce Lee and his friend and training partner Dan Inosanto during the Sixties and Seventies. A book showing this could, to an extent, be tethered to the past and that wasn't what I wanted. Like Lee, I have used a conceptual approach and I have taken many of Lee's thoughts on the nature of combat to serve, in his own words, as a finger-pointing. There is very little esoteric terminology in the book. The aim is to make it clear and simple and help you on your way to being an effective martial artist. Lee's focus was on the functionality of the technique or training method and that is my focus within this book. It is a study of fighting: only fighting. It uses some of Lee's techniques as a base and adds what is functional and desirable from modern methods and my own experience to show a way that is relevant to modern martial artists.

Scope of the book

In this book I cover primarily empty hands (as opposed to weapon-based) fighting, and stand-up rather than grappling fighting. Sparring, close-quarter fighting, knife defence, stick fighting and grappling are outside the scope of this book but crucial nevertheless to developing a rounded fighting skillset. Similarly, I do not cover areas like training kit, or warming up and down, stretches or conditioning training, but the importance of these cannot be overstated. My aim is to walk the line between function and technique, execution and strategy.

My background

My own interest in strategy and principles began before I had heard of Bruce Lee or Dan Inosanto. I lost my first fight at the age of five and remember thinking 'what's this all about?' I was soon to learn! I had lots of fights as I grew up, something that I thought was normal, yet for lots of modern youngsters is alien. Over time I got much better at fighting, yet a number of specific fights made me want to understand the theory and practice of fighting even more. In one I fought a boxer and lost not on heart, as I had plenty, but on lack of technique. I had no method to apply. Another school fight involved a whole transition from group threat to single unarmed combat, then knife against my empty hands, and then a bottle attack, all the time surrounded by a group. Maybe that's why I have had a life-long interest in weaponry and how to defend against it. Another found me at a rugby match, fighting all of the opposing team of fifteen with only a friend for assistance. These were great inspirations to learn more. I was no great hero, as I wanted a quiet life like everyone else, but circumstances dictated that I fought fairly frequently and had close friends who were involved in fighting a lot of the time. Just being in this down-to-earth environment meant I got to see and experience a lot of scenarios first-hand.

The Peter O'Donnell books about his fictional hero Modesty Blaise were around and popular before I heard of Bruce Lee. O'Donnell's characters showed great use of strategy and techniques and their fighting was, in a sense, like JKD before JKD had been invented. To a young man practising Karate they were yet another source of inspiration to gain more knowledge and understand the game more thoroughly. In my Karate practice I had been fortunate to come under the tutelage of Tatsuo Suzuki 7th Dan. This took me off the street corner. Now I was a Karate practitioner, a stoic monk-like character in my own mind. My whole life filled up with Karate and I became one of the UK's first black belts as, back then, the Karate scene here was very small. Karate was for me life-fulfilling; I had found what I wanted to do yet had no interest in teaching: training was my life. However, a reluctant one-time job, taking the place of a Japanese instructor who was ill, led me to find the thing I was destined to do for the rest of my life.

Teaching others and training were my new existence. Karate was great but at that time the world was changing. In the late 1960s doors previously closed were opening everywhere. I trained with top Judo players and boxers and loved to grapple even though my Karate friends thought it unseemly. Meetings and exchanges with Kung Fu practitioners also happened around this time whilst I was working as a stuntman and I gained more fight knowledge from working the doors. During this time we were all adapting, when into this matrix came Bruce Lee. Much of what we read about Bruce in the magazines we already knew. My training partners and I used a boxing stance and did hand immobilizations and many of the other things that were talked about in these articles on Bruce. However, my visits to Chinatown's Chinese movie theatres to see him in action made me aware that he was on another level entirely. I was a convert overnight and devoured anything about him or anything he wrote. Much of it resonated with my own experiences. I loved his use of training equipment and was intrigued by the wooden dummy. We took what we could and fought full contact and gained a rough and ready experience. I was also studying Okinawan weaponry from my friend John Sullivan who I'd been in Japan with. It all went into the mix and refined my knowledge.

My own development has been helped incredibly by training with incredible people. When I first saw Tatsuo Suzuki in action I knew that I wanted to do what he was doing. Through him I learnt to be stoical and to adapt my game to my body. He had a bad back injury so found it hard to kick high with ease, yet was still a very potent fighter. From Hisaomi Fuji, All Japan Karate Champion, I learnt not only about timing and counter-punching but also about being a gentleman and having empathy with those who trained with me and under me. I owe him a great debt. My continuing enthusiasm was fed by Tadayuki Maeda, another All Japan champion, and, on film, by another champion, Iida, who unfortunately I never met in person. Further, multi-faceted inspiration came from meeting Don Draeger in

Japan. I saw in him how to behave as a true martial artist, constantly enquiring but self-controlled and humble.

Boxing has also been instrumental in my development. I was forbidden to box at school when I was young because of an ear operation which meant I couldn't pass the medical. As a result of this ban I have boxed or fought continually ever since. Additionally, my love affair with good boxing had been fostered as a youth when I worked at the London Hilton for my father. He organised the catering for all the top boxing matches. Through this I met and talked to boxing greats like Jack Dempsey and Joe Louis. I met them all, many great fighters and some great men. They all left an impression.

Foremost among all I have trained with is Dan Inosanto, Bruce Lee's training partner. My initial meeting with him in 1979 was amazing and blew me, and my friends, away. It showed me that there was much more to learn and that I had better get going.

I have been privileged to train with Dan for nearly thirty years and I am one of his longest-serving students, though probably not his best. We have moved from a master-student relationship to one

where he is friend, mentor, and master but above all a constant inspiration. Dan has encouraged my study of various martial ways and I have had great success in many of these. Meeting Dan has changed my life, as he has changed the lives of countless others.

The training partners I have had along the way have been an invaluable aid to my development and my understanding of martial arts. Foremost amongst these during the Seventies and Eighties must be Ralph Jones and Geoff Britton. We were the band of brothers who travelled and fought together. Ralph became my soul brother when we moved into JKD. He was the ying to my yang and we spent days talking about concepts and strategies. Like me he shared a love of Modesty Blaise books. In recent years my training has been enlivened by an amazing group of training partners and friends. I owe a great debt to all of them: Terry Barnett, who started training with me over thirty years ago, Neil McLeod, David Onuma, Wayne Rowlands, Owen Ogbourne, Dave Birkett, Steve Wright, another long time student and friend Alex Turnbull and my inspirational old friends Alex Livingstone and Ian Oliver. Finally I should mention my close friend and student Lou Manzi who I get to work out all my theories on and who serves as my training dummy. In recent times, arthritis limited my game until I had two hip replacements, from which I recovered with the help of some great training with James Evans Nichol in Submission Wrestling and in Silat with Steve Benitez and his team.

Learning to fight: the process

The progression for anyone learning any art tends to follow the same pattern. This is how we describe it in my instructor training program and for our phased training program:

> Build a base
> Seek the method
> Become the method
> Abandon the method
> Return to simplicity

To go through all these stages in every aspect of the arts is a lifetime's study. Many of us are at different stages of development in various areas of the art. Only once you truly understand can you feel free to abandon the method and go with what the situation dictates. Any art that allows you at an early stage to express your own ideas and your 'way,' which encourages improvisation around a theme or simple concept, whilst also emphasizing quality basics will, I believe, allow you to achieve some mastery of your art. Of course, mastery is always a relative term; as you get better the level of expectancy just gets higher.

Build a base

In all arts the highest levels of achievement are built upon mastery of the fundamentals. Sound knowledge of the basics is essential both in self-defence and for sparring. At this level it's about repetition and building body knowledge. It's my belief that good boxing and kickboxing skills will give you the core of your fight game and put you in a position to use more advanced trapping (reacting to your opponent's energy to manipulate and pin, or 'trap,' the limbs) or grappling skills to finish if you so choose. You can fight just using trapping and grappling, but they work better when supplanted by a boxing or kickboxing base. Good boxing skills also build confidence and courage and make you more at ease in a chaotic situation. This is a core part of developing your game.

Seek the method

Once you have an understanding of a basic game, you can start to learn more about the method and the techniques involved, plus you start to pick up on the subtleties of the art and build basic technique in depth. You start to gain the understanding and positional knowledge to be able to use the more esoteric techniques within the art. Along with technique this is a time to place great emphasis on learning timing and distance – something you should work hard to develop. This is a time of research and study.

Become the method

At this level you are in the art. You know the techniques and now are in a practising mode, refining your skills and learning where things happen. In sparring at this level or even earlier you will find the many reference points, as Lee called them; the common positions where you often find yourself. From these reference points you have numerous techniques available, and you have a base or common entry point for improvising or relating to your opponent's energy. By using reference points your improvisation skills are based around common themes and start points, and chaos doesn't seem so chaotic. You don't choose beforehand what you are going to do; rather, you go with the flow, relating to your opponent and what they choose to do, responding with the appropriate technique.

Abandon the method

When you can consistently flow, you are starting to abandon the method – you are on the road to mastering or transcending your art. It's first about gaining a deep knowledge of the fundamentals, then adapting them to your body and to your experience. You create your way, based on the past but not limited by it. It's just fighting. When you are at this level you have no expectation of how things will be; you just go with what is, taking it as it comes.

Return to simplicity

This book is mainly concerned with giving you a toolkit of techniques and an understanding of where they fit time-wise and distance-wise: a basic why, what and when of fighting. Once you have really mastered and internalised the techniques you can start to interrogate them, selecting and developing those which work best for you, throwing away those that don't and unconsciously fighting. You eventually come full circle, back to where, as Bruce Lee said, 'a punch is just a punch, a kick just a kick.'

Looking at this process from the beginning you can see that you will first have to learn what the attack or defence looks like. This is when you are building a base. Next, you start to use your growing recognition of shape and movement, often without any knowledge of how things fit together. It's a 'let's try this' type of approach if you're attacking, and a reactive approach if you're defending. This is where you build your experience. There is no short cut here. To research your experience you have to have some, so this means sparring, drilling and learning as you go. Eventually you get to the point, when you've done lots of repetition in drilling and sparring, where you can see the shape of the coming attack. Alternatively, you construct a situation where the person is likely to do the thing you want. The highest point of the art is where you can force your opponent to do what you want whether he is aware of it or not. Of course the ultimate aim of martial arts is to forestall any belligerence on a potential opponent's part, before it even gets started, by your spiritual and physical presence.

Because of my early fight experiences, throughout all of my training and teaching it has been the dichotomy between being functional whilst also being 'within the art' that has intrigued me. Being 'within the art' can also mean being chaotic – but in a knowing way. I had tried a naïve, yet chaotic, approach in my youth and found that I just got more bruises that way. To paraphrase the poet Oliver Wendell Holmes, I don't want the simplicity on this side of complexity, I want the simplicity on the *other* side of complexity. The aim is to 'be' in the moment; as Bruce Lee would say, 'responding like an echo.' This can only be done with a good knowledge of the fundamentals; that doesn't mean only knowing what the fundamentals look like and being able to perform them parrot-fashion. This is the trap that a minority of Karate practitioners fell into (though to my mind that isn't the real Karate). 'If it looks good it must be good,' is the ethos of this type of training. This is OK at a base level and we all have to go through this. Then it's on to really understanding your tools and being able to dictate to or flow with your opponent, using basic tools with variety and finesse.

This process, I think, can be accelerated if you know what you are doing and where you are going. Bruce was the first in the modern era to look at combat this way and we should respect his genius in this. He was an innovator and has changed the face of modern martial arts worldwide.

How to use this book

This book covers basic technique first, then moves on to more advanced technique and finally considers some of the more strategic elements of fighting. If you are a novice then you first need to get a good grounding in the fundamentals. I have given training routines which will help your progress. If you are more experienced or seek to understand the timing aspects mentioned throughout the text then take a look at the fighting time line in chapter 15 and keep that in mind whilst reading the rest of the book. Think about how you can use the concepts of 'before, during and after' to good effect. Look at ways you can advance your techniques up the time line so they are more pro-active rather than reactive. Realise too that sometimes appearing to be slow and behind the beat is often just as effective as being ahead of the beat as long as you are not being hit. An understanding of opening and closing lines is essential if you are to make the most of your opportunities. Research your own experience, look at where on the line you do most of your work and adapt it so you have more depth and understanding.

I'm also going to assume a left lead – apologies to the southpaws out there. If you're just starting out I normally recommend that you put your left side forwards if you are right-handed. However, both sides work and both have advantages. As you advance, you should be training all techniques on both sides. If you've got the time it's immaterial which side you start out on. However, I've seen a lot of great fighters who don't have this depth and only fight from one side. Therefore there are two approaches to training martial arts; one is a fighting-only approach where generally simple works best, the other is a combined fighting and bodily health approach. Choose whichever approach best suits you.

Notes

Throughout the book, for convenience I use the male pronoun instead of the wordier 'his or her' each time. Apologies to anyone who thinks I'm being sexist – if you knew some of the female black belts at my Academy you'll know I'm under no illusion about the efficacy and competence of many female fighters.

You should also use this book in conjunction with professionally-instructed classes. There is no substitute for a good teacher and you should go out of your way to seek one out.

Finally, make sure at all times that you respect and take care of your training partners. Ensure you approach your training with focus and passion, but be thoughtful and considerate too.

Part 1: Preparation

01: Stance

'Float like a butterfly, sting like a bee.' Drew Bundini Brown

In this chapter we will cover basic stances: how to use them, and how to move around, flowing between them, whilst keeping well-balanced. The trick to fighting is to hit hard without getting hit at the same time. Therefore, you need to be well balanced, rooted at the point of impact so that you can deliver blows with force, whilst at the same time being mobile so that you aren't a fixed target.

Stances are not techniques themselves; they help you to execute a particular technique and so they shouldn't get in the way of it. Neither are they fixed poses; rather, a stance is like a still from a movie, a snapshot of part of a movement that isn't stiff or fixed. Stances are shapes that you move through whilst fighting and are bases for you to launch attacks from.

When you first start to learn how to fight, you use stances as a handy reference point and you have to learn them well. As you progress, you learn to improvise around them and they become transitional. Ultimately, you forget them. It's about learning where your balance is, and learning how to move between stances or to move using the same stance. Using stances at this early stage helps you to develop good footwork and to find out how to hit effectively whilst remaining mobile.

Simple stance changes can have a profound impact on your opponent's ability to strike effectively. The most suitable thing to do is often dictated by your opponent, so you must remain flexible and able to move with good balance in all directions with ease. With all stances and footwork, keep your striking and kicking tools directed towards your opponent.

Front stance

The front stance is the basic stance used in boxing. The weight is forward on the lead foot and the rear heel is raised. The body is slightly turned so that you offer a smaller target, and the hands are held high and tight to cover against blows. Note also that they are in an offensive position directed at the opponent, not pointed upwards, which would show your opponent that you are defensive and no danger to them. This is really important: it's essential that you are the hunter and not the hunted. Your body inclination and direction should show this in no uncertain terms: offence is the best defence. The raised rear heel is crucial as this will allow you to move backwards easily. This can be done temporarily with 'snapback' (see page 78) where you move and then come back to your attack, or it can be a more permanent type of footwork move.

Front stance

Pros and cons

It's an easy stance to learn and use. It provides a great platform for delivering hand blows in particular, and leg strikes at longer distances. In the front stance, lead kicks are normally done with a step or slide. Even though this might telegraph your intentions, if the step and slide are disguised with a hand strike or a feint they work well. The extended front leg is vulnerable to attack either from round kicks or tackles. Therefore, when using it, flow in and out of it using a shorter Thai stance (see below) as your neutral stance. Be aware of tackle attempts and keep light and mobile so that you can respond easily. This front stance is the best one from which to use hand strikes, rather than kicks.

Thai stance

This is a shorter, more neutral stance used commonly in Thai boxing. Place your feet so that the back of the heel of your lead foot lines up with the toes of your back foot. You can make this stance slightly longer at times, but it is normally kept quite short. Make sure that the hips are raised and both heels are up. Your body is fairly square as your first line of defence is your legs; protecting your centre line isn't so important. If your opponent attacks, you can keep him at bay using kicks and long knees, then integrate hands into this mix. Hands can often be out in a long guard; these extended hands serve a multitude of purposes. They can keep your opponent at a kicking or kneeing range; they can be used very effectively to parry your opponent's blows at their origin; they can be used to grab your opponent and bring him into a clinch position, thus killing his boxing range; and you can use your hands to mask your opponent's face so that he can't see whilst you attack.

Pros and cons

The Thai stance is great for kicking. You are compact, with good balance, so that you can use the legs easily for low-line defence, either by crushing, or by striking. The squarer position means that you can kick easily to wide angles, though it is not so good at long range. The hands can still be effective but because of the raised heel stance, punches tend to be weaker unless you drive from the ankles, which are kept hard and strong. The long guard can be vulnerable to your opponent coming underneath it with hand attacks, though this isn't a problem if your knee techniques are good.

Thai stance

Lateral stance / Yee kim ma

The lateral stance is used at close range. It differs from the boxing and Thai approach in that the head is further back. Though this isn't the best stance for delivering very powerful blows, it is highly effective in a self-defence mode or when you don't want to escalate what may just be a tussle into an all-out fight. It gives you a scaleable defence. Taught more formally in Wing Chun styles, this stance, in a looser format, is also used by Filipino Kali and Indonesian Silat systems. Open your legs as shown by rotating the toes outwards first, then pivoting the heels out further. This will give you the standard stance. However, it can be looser than this, just as long as you understand the principle. One leg has seventy percent of the weight and the other thirty. When attacked on one angle you adjust your weight and move to the other angle; it means you have an attacking angle on your opponent.

Pros and cons

Elusive and very functional, the lateral stance can be used to stay out of the way, passively, of opponents' blows, or can be made much more aggressive with the use of blows like the straight blast or chain punching which is hard to counter at close range. To be most effective, the ability to flow from this to boxing or clinching and standing grappling is essential. It requires good hand skills to be most effective and only works well at close range.

These are some of the basic stances which we will work with in this book. They are just the basic building blocks and should be well practised. Add these to the footwork drills in chapter 3 and develop an awareness of your own body's balance and movement.

Lateral stance

02: Range and Measure

Range and measure, alongside timing, are of the utmost importance in fighting. You have to know when you are out of the range of his kicks and punches, or at what range you can most effectively use your various kicks and punches – your body tools. Phrases like 'I've got the measure of him' have their origins in the combative notions of measure and range in sword fighting. This is not only a weapon concept; it is just as applicable to empty hands.

Understanding ranges

There are four basic ranges: long range, medium range, close range and ground fighting. They inform the stances that you move through and the techniques you select. Sometimes techniques work in all three standing ranges. Don't see ranges as fixed measures – they blur and overlap – but dividing the space around you into ranges is a useful way to lay the foundation of your understanding and make it easier for you to learn techniques and concepts. When you have real ability, you flow from range to range without thought as you respond and react.

Long range

When you and your opponent are just out of each other's reach, you would need to step in to use any of your attacks effectively. You either want to draw him in or use methods to bridge the gap. You use your longest spear-like tools – including lead side kicks, front kicks and jabs – to both measure your distance and to get closer to him where you can use your more effective, destructive tools.

Find your measure with a jab

Medium range

Medium range is where much martial arts training takes place and as a result it's where the inexperienced fighter might want to be – not too close, not too far away. However, at this range your opponent can deliver all of his tools most effectively and may be feeling his most comfortable. It's a dangerous range and has to be well trained. Here you need good skills to stay and fight, plus the ability to go closer and restrict your opponent's chance to unload by tying him up, locking him, or alternatively taking him down. The other alternative is to be able to move easily into the long range with the minimum of effort, then be ready to come in again when the opportunity presents itself.

Close range

At close range there is a lot of potential for things to happen. Both you and your opponent have most of your tools available and you can manipulate, grapple and tie your opponent up, in addition to striking. This range thus has many games and approaches which include boxing; clinch, knee and elbow; trapping; standing grappling and throwing; and locking.

Ground fighting

Although outside the scope of this book, the ground fighting range is a crucial area to master since many fights end up on the floor. Don't neglect its training.

Finding your measure

Your measure is the furthest distance at which your tools work well against your opponent. First you have to learn your measure. Once that's done, it's easier

for you to know your opponent's, so that with a minimum of movement you can be just out of range.

First, you have to know your measure with the jab and the lead leg side kick, your longest tools. Then you can go on to understand how to increase your workable distance by adding different types of step or lunge. It's very easy to understand both your own and your opponent's range and measure once you've got one fixed distance of measure, much like using a ruler.

In the picture (left) you can see my hand measure with a jab (if it's a finger jab I just add four inches). I make sure that I stretch even to the point of being nearly off balance so that I know the furthest extent of my reach. If my opponent is at a longer range I do the same jab but with an initial step, and over time I get to know the length of my step. I then mentally know that I will be able to hit my opponent if he's within my measure or my measure plus a step. If he's further, I know he's in kicking range, firstly of the rear leg and then the lead leg. I get to know the furthest range from which my tools still hit and then just add the different steps, depending on how much ground I have to cover.

It seems complicated, but the place to start is by learning the range of your tools without stepping, or with lead leg kicks, stepping within the length of your stance. Once you know this, you've got a fixed measure to which you can then add steps if you aren't close enough.

Similarly, once you know your measure you'll be better able to gauge your opponent's distance and use range defensively. You can snapback so that he misses by fractions of an inch. This makes it much easier for you to counter-attack. An alternative to making his strikes miss is drawing him in deeper. Because he's missing every time, he over-extends, then you can slip in and be so close that either he can't generate enough power or the angle is wrong for his blow to work effectively. Then you can clinch or manipulate his balance. In these ways you destroy his confidence. Often he hits air or can't unload and you are in the right place to knock him down or out.

I spar with many students who have no knowledge of their own distance, so they take unnecessary steps to get close enough. This uses too much time, and announces their intention. Don't let that be you.

Core principle: Centre line

The centre line is a crucial aspect of your understanding of the combative relationship between you and your opponent. Many of the prime targets like the groin, solar plexus, throat and chin are located along this line. Differing styles of fighting approach the defence of these areas differently. Some styles like to defend the centre line by having the arms there, so you have to get past them. However, most practical fighters leave the centre line open – it's the area where your eyes are the best defensive tools to use. Your arms are better deployed to guard against looping, hooking blows to the head, where your eyes don't work at their best. Also, in this way, you draw your opponent to attack you down the centre line – you lure him in. Bruce Lee called this 'attack by drawing.' You seem open but in reality you're ready to respond. From a defensive standpoint you've got to realise that you can't defend everywhere. If you cover the centre you're open at the edges; if you cover the edges you are open in the centre, either for chain punching or attacks up and down your centre line. Similarly, you can't effectively defend both high and low lines. What you should do is close no door too tightly; if you close one door you've only opened another on the other side. Rather, use a combination of body or head movements with a minimal blocking or parrying method to defend against any blows. Leave your centre line open but close up the nearer the fight gets to you. Think of your guard movements as a night watchman who goes round and checks all the locks periodically. It means you're not fixed in a certain position. All fixed positions eventually get overrun or the opponent goes round them. You can attack your opponent's centre line without being directly in front of him, therefore he's not able to attack your centre as effectively as you are his.

03: Footwork

Footwork training features an essential contradiction. Combatively, you need to move with the minimum of effort and only just enough for your opponent to miss and waste his energy. However, to be really competent at footwork you have to do more than is necessary in the training stage so that you get to the point where your body loves to move. Most people in class would like to stand where they are, thus it's essential that you overdo the mobility thing in the beginning. This will also, of course, keep you very fit and is great exercise.

Therefore make sure that you exaggerate your use of footwork in training. Get to the point where you love to move and that this is your standard response when working the pads or shadow-boxing. Then, when fighting, you should make sure that you don't do too much, as sometimes closing one door just opens another. See this as first learning the skill, then refining the skill. Only use what you need.

Boxing series footwork

Step and slide

The first type of footwork to learn is the step and slide. This is the standard way of adjusting your position in relation to an opponent so that you can stay at a consistent distance. This is normally the point at which you are at the end of his range and the beginning of yours and where both of you can hit with your hands if you take a step forward. You move the leg nearest to the direction you are going first, and slide the other one after it, so that you are back in your standard stance. This can be done forwards and back and left and right. Moving right is the most difficult and you have to take smaller steps – there are a number of other options for moving right that are more functional (see L step, p.26).

Slide and step

The slide and step can be used to maintain your range in relation to your opponent when the gap is slightly larger or you have to make up distance. Alternatively it's great when accompanied by strikes which hide the footwork. Slide your back foot up towards your front foot then take a step with your leading foot. When going backwards, slide the front foot back, and then take a step backwards with your rear foot. Don't bob up and down: keep your head at a constant level. A variation on this theme is to raise the closest leg like a crush or jamming technique. When going forwards it can be used to jam your opponent's attack attempt, and when going back it can be used to crush your opponent's attack or counter-attack.

Step and slide

Slide and step

Shuffle bounce

By bouncing on your toes you will find it easy to go in any direction. You can't get huge changes in distance with this type of footwork unless you lunge in with the lead foot, which isn't difficult from here. The shuffle makes you light and elusive and makes it difficult for your opponent to know which direction you are going to go in.

Shuffle bounce

Pivot

Fix your lead leg to the floor and pivot around it. It's incredible how functional this can be at close range as it destroys much of the body shifting that your opponent has worked so hard for. By pivoting you keep your tools focused on your opponent and withdraw yourself out of effective range of the attack. When going clockwise you can use both hand tools well; when going the other way the cross sometimes seems easier.

The pivot nullifying an attempted hook

Lateral triangle

This is another type of footwork where one limb is fixed and you move around it. Used commonly in stick fighting and in Jun Fan, where it's called Toy Gerk, it works well as either a temporary adjustment or, when you move your lead leg out of harm's way, it can be made deeper and eventually lead to a stance change. As such there are about three depths at which you can do this. This can initially be seen as a technique but really it's about you reacting to your opponent's attacks and responding accordingly.

Lateral triangle

Curve left and right

Curving left and right takes you out of harm's way against an opponent trying to trap you in a corner or against side attacks like the round kick. It can also keep you out of the centre line focus that your opponent wants because that's where he can charge or lunge in most effectively. Being just off his centre line all the time means that you are stealing time from him yet keeping your own attacking options open. Practise curving either in shadow-boxing or when doing pad work (the feeder can give you slow round kicks or wide hooks to get you to move off-line at the end of your combinations). You don't need to move too far, just far enough that you are off the centre. Watch good Cuban boxers and you'll see this used to great effect. Don't be there, waiting to get hit.

L-step (Switch)

Withdraw your lead leg and step to the right with your rear leg. It has a sort of skipping feel to it. Once you've switched you can either replace your lead foot on a parallel line to the initial one or you can walk in an arc and reinstate your stance anywhere on the arc. This footwork gets you out of the range of his big right hand punch and is an easier way to move to the right than the step and slide or curve.

Around the pad drill

This is the first type of footwork drill we teach at my Academy. It's easy, and connects foot and brain quickly and instinctively. You can see this as a stance change done at distance so that you change from an orthodox to a southpaw lead, either when attacked or when you decide that it is a good thing to do. Once again it makes you light and elusive.

Step through

This is a different stance change but this time it is performed at medium to close range. Often used in Filipino boxing, it immediately puts pressure on your opponent's balance. Often we do this either with a crushing or trapping technique as shown, or when your hit falls short and you just follow it in, because if you try to pull it out you will get what Bruce Lee called 'hang time' where you're lingering at the end of a blow.

Therefore you can see that it is possible to change stance at long range, as in going round the pad, or at close range where you are making the most of a bad position and crashing inwards. Both work well and can mess up your opponent.

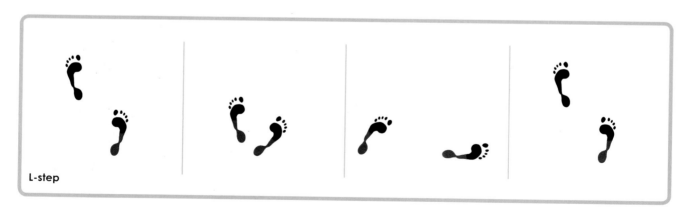

L-step

Going around the pad

Summary

It's important to note that you can either move your feet or move your body to evade; it's difficult to do both at the same time. So when working evasion, use footwork as one method, and body evasion from a fixed stance as the second method. Eventually you will flow between them so seamlessly that most people won't see that it's two different approaches. We'll look at body evasion later on in Part 3.

Step through

04: Guards

The guard is the position that your hands will be held in whilst you move and fight. You want to cover as much of your body as possible, and to do this it's helpful to visualise the body divided into quadrants as shown below. There are four types of guards that you need to know which we'll look at in this chapter.

Quadrants

Standard guard

Standard guard

This is where your forearms are held vertical, like two pillars. Point your hands towards your opponent, elbows in, body turned to offer less of a target. The rear hand covers the rear quadrant, the lead hand covers the lead upper quadrant and the elbows cover the side rear and lead quadrants.

Half guard

Use the half guard when you are at medium or close range. It is often easier to bob and weave with the lead arm dropped. Here, the lead arm is in a

position to lead hook and can also be used as a bar across your opponent's body used to push him off balance or jam him so he can't use his hands, which is particularly effective if he is using the standard guard. Use the shoulder roll (p. 82) and bob and weave (p.78-79) to cover against right hand blows.

Cross guard

The cross guard is versatile and can be used in a variety of ways. Firstly, use it to crush your opponent's blows (p. 75). Secondly, it's a great way to cover whilst actively bobbing and weaving. Make sure

Half guard

Cross guard

both hands are fully cocked to enable a left or right hook; you can easily trap his limbs as your hand grabs are there for easy use. It is easy to flow into the cross guard from the half guard; often the two guards flow from one to the other in use. The only rule is 'don't get hit.' Remember that the cross guard and the half guard don't work particularly well at long distances and can leave you open to simple trapping. Body movement and closing your opponent down are essential parts of both these guards.

Long guard

The long guard is used in Thai boxing and Filipino Kali. Either, or both, hands can be extended. This exposes the ribs but the added risk can be worth it as it's much easier to manipulate your opponent at the origin of his blows and kicks. You can body-

check him to reduce his kicking power and use the extended lead to head grab and eliminate his boxing range. You can also manipulate his head to offset his balance or use your thumb to gouge his eye.

Long guard

Checking the doors

Guards aren't fixed, even though they might look like that in the photos. Take the standard guard as an example. The lead hand should pulse towards your opponent so that when you do jab, the first part of it is hidden from him, disguised in a sea of constant motion. Similarly, move the rear hand as if you're cleaning a window. Touch your forehead occasionally to make sure that your hands are up (it's so easy to drop them, so make this a habit) and sometimes, briefly, withdraw it to a half-guard position. This means your opponent has to watch for your jab; he can get the cross in only occasionally because you're monitoring your cover with a head touch and he can't reliably predict that your hand will be there to be trapped. Add level change to this, using your knees whilst keeping your head up, and head movement as well as evasion. This means your head is moving up and down in addition to evading left and right, instantly reducing your hitability. Keep the elbows tight, though they can sometimes go forwards to cut his angles off for any potential body strikes. The rear hand can make little circles and occasionally go forwards in a vague trapping attempt when not threatening his line with a cross or other blow.

Above all, threaten your opponent: don't think defensively but always threaten to take the game to him so that he is more hesitant and is stopped before he builds up momentum.

Also, change guards and game occasionally as he will be planning his response to your standard game while you're fighting. Doing a big change can keep your opponent mentally unbalanced and not in control of the fight. Similarly, sometimes withdraw from the conflict totally. Don't engage; then at a time of your choice go back in with intent. Vary the rhythm of the fight by changing guard, changing footwork, changing distance and changing power – light and evasive then hunting down with power blows. It makes it very hard for your opponent to deal with and puts you in charge of what's happening.

Remember all of this is built on simple basics. Learn those first; then rotate them in your training; then integrate them into your game. Be the hunter.

In Part One I've covered stances, footwork and guards and introduced the concepts of range, distance and the centre line. In Part Two we'll look at strikes and kicks to use from the mobile base we've created.

Part Two: Attack

05: Punches

Principles of striking

I see many students at my Academy who are very muscular yet can't hit hard. It shows that good striking ability isn't based solely on muscular strength but rather on good body mechanics: hitting using all of your body, using as many levers acting together as possible. It's even more important that you hit using your skeleton, not just your muscles. Make contact with your opponent with the bones of your body lined up behind the strike, so that there are a minimum number of joints having to be held in place by gross muscular force. As one of my old friends used to say, 'where there's a joint, there's a weakness.' Throughout Part Two I will show you how to line your body up for maximum effectiveness. It means you will punch above your weight and it will put you in the 'big hitters' league.

Punches

The jab

The jab was accurately described by Bruce Lee and many fighters before him as the mark of the expert. The jab is inherently simple, yet its use can be very varied and very destructive. To think of the jab as just an opening or ranging shot is to only understand one aspect of it.

The basic jab

Stand in the basic front stance with both hands up. The rear hand is near the corner of the jaw and the lead hand is on or near the centre line with the elbow tucked in. Push with the back leg, in particular from the raised-heel rear foot. Turn the hand so it is palm downward en route to making contact. Remember to hit with the first two knuckles of the hand and hold the fist tight with the thumb. On contact your body should form a straight line going from the fist, across your back, and down to the rear foot. Move your head slightly forwards and off-line to the right so that even though you deliver the jab quickly you are still hitting with all of your body's weight. As you're stacking your body up in a straight line behind your punch, you will find that you are less likely to crumble if you hit a heavy opponent.

Starting position

Whilst your lead hand should generally start from a standard guard position, remember this isn't fixed. Circle the hand both clockwise and anti-clockwise and pulse it towards your opponent – it means your jab has various starting points and makes the timing of the attack harder for your opponent to forecast.

Ways to practise the jab

First practise the jab on the spot, without moving your feet, as we saw in Chapter 2: by leaning your body in you can learn how far away you can be whilst still able to hit. Add a lead step, if you need the extra depth to hit the target. The hand should move first or at the same time as the foot.

Double jab

Again, first practise the double jab from a fixed position so you use the correct body mechanics. Let the power for the second punch come from a bounce in the legs. Once you can do this well, practise with a step. The double jab is for penetrating deep into your opponent's defence, for putting him on the back foot and possibly to set up the cross. Take a step forward on the second jab, making sure that you move the hand before the foot. Once again, don't get the power for the second jab from the arm; rather, almost spring from the legs so that the arm needs to do the minimum of work. Work on making the second jab as hard, if not harder, than the first but with little effort – the power should come from the legs and correct body alignment. Bring the hand back quickly to its starting position after the second strike. Don't drop your hand or let it curve inwards as your opponent will then have an open line along which to strike. Keep your rear hand open and near the corner of your jaw; keep your elbows in and your head down.

Other jabs

It's a good idea to work a number of variations to the jab. First let's look at the stiff jab, best done when you are retreating. Line the body up and, as you punch, allow less snap in the muscles and joints than with the regular jab. Instead, lock your arm for a fraction of a second; think of it like a fixed scaffold pole. You should feel the shock of the punch go down into your rear foot. The stiffness of this blow prevents your opponent from coming forwards.

Next there is the flicker jab. This is the opposite of the stiff jab: here you want to just flick the jab out. Make sure your body is lined up properly if you can, but this jab can still be thrown when you're unprepared. Use the flicker jab to gain intelligence about your opponent's intention – it gives you instant feedback about his thinking. Also use it as a fake to draw his guard high so that you can come in underneath. The surprise nature of this jab makes your opponent overreact.

The standing fist jab is used when your opponent has a very tight guard. Keep the elbow in and the fist strong, with the palm to the side. Drive from the legs. This is a great way to interrogate the centre line and often sets up the left hook really well as your opponent tends to close the centre tightly.

The best method is to mix all the jabs together. Flick for distance and presence then change the power so that suddenly it's a really heavy strike. Mix in doubles and the stiff jab as your opponent starts to respond. Change tempo and power characteristics too, and you have a potent strategy.

Jab

The cross and straight right

Rear-hand punches are amongst the most powerful tools you have. As shorthand when teaching, we often refer to both the cross and the straight right punches as the 'cross.' However, the cross is a punch which loops around the opponent's guard, whereas the straight right goes directly through a hole in the centre of the guard. Here we are going to deal with them as separate punches, but they share similar body mechanics.

Straight right

To deliver this punch, turn your body as if the left hand side of your body is a hinge. Rotate on the toes of the rear foot and turn the shoulders. Move your head off-line, forward and to the left. Make the hand travel in a straight line; don't let the elbow come out too much or it's easy for your opponent to see the punch coming, and then to block or stifle it. It's important to hit with the whole body so be sure you form a line going from your fist to your rear foot. Have the rear knee pointing in the direction that you are hitting and don't let it twist too much to the left. Make sure all your levers are lined up and throwing the punch forwards.

Cross

Cross

Whereas the straight right is intended to spear straight through the opponent's guard, the cross is meant to go across and around his guard, as the name implies. The cross, like the right hook, can be very hard to deal with as it penetrates your guard at an unusual angle. However, if defending against it, a change of distance can often make it miss and go across the front of you. Let the rear knee follow the direction of the punch but remember to have all your levers lined up so that they add power to the blow.

As with the jab, there are different types of cross and straight right. Your degree of commitment to the punch can change depending on the circumstances. Concentrate, so that there is no telegraphing of the punch: no wind-up or clenching of the fist to show your opponent that it's coming. Some boxers, like Mohammed Ali, use this almost like a jab; others, like Mike Tyson, use their straight right and cross like missiles. Use both methods to understand the tool: practise with minimal commitment where the cross is fast and snappy and then with greater commitment by throwing your body weight behind the punch. Also, practise punching with the arm leading and the body following and supporting the blow, then do the opposite: move the body first and then dispatch the arm. You'll make the timing of your blow much harder to read.

It is worth remembering that the rear hand punch can be thrown at a variety of angles. It can help to think of this as hitting at various numbers on a clock face. If seen from your perspective, punch straight and hit towards the six o'clock. Then hit at five o'clock, four o'clock, three o'clock and so on. It makes you practise putting your hand into the holes in your opponent's guard. This method can be extended until you are hitting directly overhead in a looping hit that descends, bang on twelve o'clock, onto your opponent's head.

Jab and cross

When moving from the jab to the cross in a combination, you will need to move the lead foot out to the left side. If you move the foot to the side as you make the jab, then you are set up for the cross and you haven't telegraphed your intention to your opponent.

The hook

The hook is one of the best punches in boxing because it comes from outside of your opponent's eye line and allows him little time to prepare himself. As they say, 'It's the punch you don't see that knocks you out.'

The standard lead hook is often thrown in a retreating manner, drawing your opponent deeper into your defensive ring. Bruce Lee used the term 'attack by drawing' to describe this form of attack. He made it one of his 'five ways of attack,' an innovative set of principles to help students to understand the concepts and structure of fighting. The secret to the hook is to first turn your body. To execute the left hook, for example, minimise your exposure by doing a shoulder roll, allowing the right shoulder to drop back: this makes you much less

Hook and forward hook

likely to get hit. Use the momentum of the turn to rotate the left hook into the target; turn your hips through 90° and let the arm follow. There are a number of ways of holding the hand and each has its benefits. The one I prefer is to make sure the fist is vertical with the palm towards you; it makes it easier to hit with your first two knuckles. If you hit with the palm down there's a greater chance you will break your hand if it isn't taped up, which it won't be in the street. Some people advocate the palm down method as it has more bite. Try both and see which suits you. Most important is to rotate the lead foot so that by the end of the punch it has moved through 90°. Your weight, when delivering the standard hook, should move to the back. Try to move the feet, rotate the body and do the punch at the same time. As your training advances, you can let the punch come with a bit of a delay which will give the hook extra whip as it tries to catch up with the rest of the body.

Forward hook

The second type of hook is the forward hook, so-called because your body weight is forward. You still rotate your body, but because the weight is on the lead foot you can't rotate it as much. However, because it's a smaller movement than the retreating hook, at close-quarter it works very well. On this hook I find the standing fist with the palm towards you works best. Don't rotate towards the rear; instead, bring the weight forwards, as it adds more bite to the punch. Feel it through your two main knuckles. Remember, the idea is to drop your opponent in one punch, so your punches have to have weight, power and bite. Make sure the elbow is in a line behind the hand on contact with your opponent. Be careful to let everything line up at the moment you make contact, without telegraphing your intention by raising the elbow too early.

A good way to practise the mechanics of the hook is by training it in conjunction with the cross. Make sure that you penetrate deeply on the cross and then rotate your lead foot, close your body as you retreat with a shoulder roll, and complete the hook.

What is important in this drill is to make the difference between the end position of the cross and that of the hook as great as possible. Do this drill hundreds of times in a constant motion without pausing at each end until you get the hook to really work well. Let the body mechanics of the cross build up the body tension to pay for the hook. It will mean that you get two for the price of one. Once you have it, you can just adapt that feel to whatever type of hook you are using.

Uppercut

Used at close range, the uppercut can be hard to stop. Slip in either direction and line your body up as shown. For the ultimate in power it's important to stack your body parts one on top of the other so that the foot-knee-hip-elbow-fist line is as straight as possible. Alternatively, lean back (whilst keeping balanced), bring your hips forward and swing upwards. Use the uppercut as part of a combination where you search for the opponent's head from a variety of angles and, as he attempts to slip, you hit him.

Uppercut

Shovel hook

Made famous by boxers like Jack Dempsey, the shovel hook can be used to the body or to the face. It is strong and effective and it's easy to sneak it inside the guard. This isn't the same punch as the uppercut, though they do look similar. You can almost look at the shovel hook as an inverted cross, though at shorter range: the punch comes from the body's core with the arm doing minimal work. Slip right or left and align the body, with your elbow near your hip. Twist the body; the punch goes inwards and slightly upwards at about a 30° angle.

Shovel hook

Backhand blows

Here I've grouped backfist and hammerfist strikes together as they have a similar motion. At closer range there is little difference between the blows except for the hand shape, or hand tool, involved.

Whatever hand tool is ultimately used, begin all of these punches with a clenched fist, changing the shape of the hand only as the arm extends. I've shown specific usages that in my experience work best.

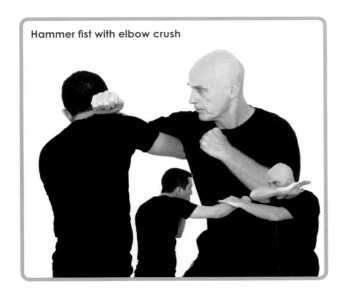

Hammer fist with elbow crush

Knifehand

Backfist

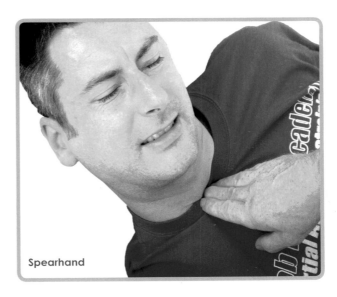

Spearhand

Long-range backfist

This should be done using the first two knuckles of the hand. The hand should be flicked out, like you would flick a towel, and whipped towards the opponent. The body should counter-rotate the other way and the weight should extend over the lead foot. This blow can often reach around the opponent's guard: if it does go through, it can be followed up with a palm heel strike or slap.

Hammerfist

Top left: elbow crush to the opponent's attacking hand before delivering the hammerfist. Right: hammer used as the opening move.

Hammer as opening move

Knifehand

The strength of the knifehand is that it will go into holes in your opponent's guard, to areas like the throat, that other blows can't reach. Also, its power-to-effort ratio is high, as the power is focused upon a small area. It's great as a half-beat strike which fills that time between major blows. Along with the spearhand, which is also usually applied to the throat, this is one of my favourite strikes but it requires really good timing and lots of repetition to make your own. There are a number of general methods for training this and the other blows, but I have chosen to show only those ones that I find work for me every day. This should help you to focus on what's functionally useful for your training.

Pak sau, half-beat throat chop

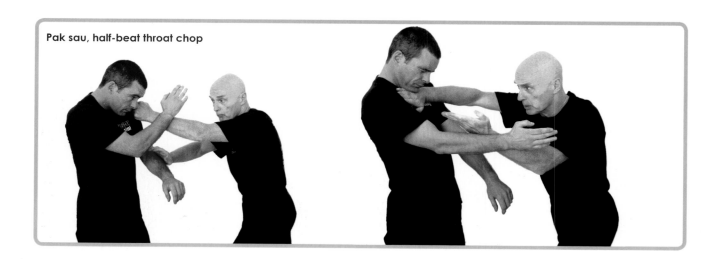

Outside parry; closest tool half-beat throat chop

Pictured below are four knifehand sequences.

Lop sau; Throat chop; Arm bar

Jau Sau; Throat chop

Spearhand

The spearhand is your longest hand tool so it makes sense to use it to good effect from a distance. Here we show it used to open up the high line which would make it easier to deliver a following kick.

Because of its small profile, it's also good at close-quarter as it fits into vulnerable areas with ease. The spearhand can be used both inside and outside of your opponent's attack. The techniques can also be done with a punch.

Split entry

Let's look at using the spearhand inside your opponent's attack, a technique often called the split entry. If your opponent attacks with jab and cross, scoop his jab away and then insert the spearhand to the throat. This works a treat and is horrible to have done to you. The forefist can be used instead of the spearhand, though my own preference is for the spearhand as it stops your opponent dead.

Open up high line with spear hand

Split entry against cross

Split entry against jab

Spearhand over cross

Outside spearhand

Below (right, previous page), we show the spearhand executed in a cutting motion over the top of both the cross and the jab. It deflects your opponent's blow and you can slide your spearhand into the eye area. Spearhand strikes don't need to have a stiff hand; rather, the hand can be kept loose so it can flow into vulnerable areas. Sometimes you can jam the fingers, so a flexible hand is needed.

Elbows

The elbow is one of your most destructive weapons at close-quarter, and it can be used in a variety of ways. Firstly, use it defensively, to crush your opponent's attack (p. 75). Secondly, it can be used to attack. This is normally achieved by making a cutting motion with the tip of the elbow. Whilst it can be used as a club, it's not so effective and is relatively easy to block which leaves you open to counters and grappling. Use the elbow where appropriate in place of the punch in the combinations throughout this book. This way you develop a close-range capability whilst still working the body mechanics for a medium and long-range game.

In addition, the elbow can be used with other strikes when in close range. For instance, when your hook misses you can let the elbow follow through and do the damage.

Counter to head control

Horizontal elbow

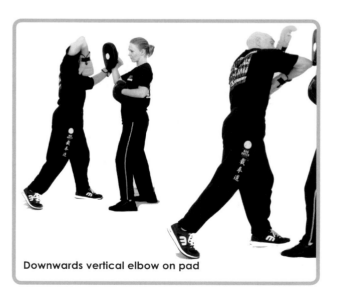

Downwards vertical elbow on pad

Training

There are numerous ways to practise the basic strikes. Start by doing everything on the spot. Make it part of your daily or weekly training routine and put the technique in your bones. Then mix the strikes up in simple combinations, as described in Chapter 7. Do repetitions, moving with the basic footwork drills between the repetitions. Do it over and over again.

Hit the bag, concentrating on just a few strikes and loop them together in singles and doubles. Make sure that there is no telegraphing of your intention. Don't be tense but let the limbs feel empty: let the strikes whip. Above all, when hitting pads or the bag, listen to the sound and make the sound the same or as similar as possible for all power strikes. The sound on your first strikes should be the same for all subsequent strikes. Let your ear lead the way.

Mix the strikes up as part of preset training drills. Shadow box using them or with a theme based around them. Mentally rehearse specific techniques: imagination is an incredible tool. Spar with a mental focus on using one tool at a time. This singularity of purpose makes you much harder to beat.

Before getting to grips with combinations it's important to understand the importance of single attacks. Getting simple single attacks to work against an opponent should be the first step in your fighting training. The idea is to land a single telling blow. It's harder than it looks and so it's a good place to start. This approach focuses on distance and timing, the two most important aspects of fighting, so it's important to get to a reasonable level in this first.

The downside of this singular approach is that you can be fixed in your position, and predictable, and you get locked into the idea of your one best shot. If your punches miss or fall short, or your opponent has an easy answer to your best shot, then your game starts to fall apart. Having a good knowledge of combinations, which we'll start to cover in Chapter 7, takes the pressure off this single game and puts pressure on your opponent.

06: Kicks and knees

Kicks are not only your longest tools but some of your most powerful. Like artillery, they allow you to do damage at a distance, yet some can also be used at very close range. The weakness in using kicks is that your balance is compromised and you can be open to being thrown. The approach that I use here is to show kicking methods which are harder for your opponent to catch, so there is a reduced threat from throws. Depending on your stance, kicks may need preparation to get your hips in the correct position under your body. This movement should be covered by fakes and high line strikes. Working from a shorter stance avoids the need for much of this preparation at middle range. At long range, you will still need to do some sort of step. Although there are stylistic differences between differing arts, when it comes to function it's best to see all of it as just kicking. Don't have a stylistic bias but focus on what's effective and what you can make work. Both snap kicks and swing kicks have a place; additionally, your own body's make-up will play a major part in defining your kicking arsenal.

Front kick

The front kick is one of the most simple yet most effective kicks for fighting. Compared to the round kick, the front kick is hard to grab and is also difficult to defend against. Here I'll show the progression that I teach in my Academy, starting with the easiest methods and then progressing to more difficult but very effective methods.

Rear leg front kick

Raise the knee and extend the leg whilst at the same time rolling the hips forward so that you make contact with all the body's weight behind the kick. Connect with the ball of the foot. Rotate the rear supporting foot slightly so that the hips are free to move. If you want, you can come up onto the ball of the supporting foot as this can give you more power; so you're 'kicking with both legs.' It's important to remember to snap the kick back and not to let it drop at the end of the attack. If you don't snap it back, it makes you open to a counter-attack because there is 'hang time' where you are hanging about at the end of your attack. Also, the extended leg is an excellent lever for your opponent to move you with if he is able to grab or scoop your kick. Get it back so that you can kick again. Don't fall in when doing the kick as this leaves you open to

Rear leg front kick

simple counters and your forward momentum adds to your opponent's power.

Lead leg front kick

There are a variety of ways of doing the lead front kick.

Pendulum step kick

The first method I teach is with a pendulum-style one-step kick. From a front stance, and while keeping your head in the same place throughout, slide your rear foot up towards the lead foot, twisting it slightly so that the heels are close together. Raise the lead leg and execute the front kick. Then replace the kicking leg back where it started and move the rear leg backwards. The movement has a pendulum-style feel to it, hence the name. If you wish to gain further distance the method I teach is to move the lead foot forwards and then to execute the pendulum step.

However, if your stance is short, as shown here, you have to step past your lead leg to kick. If your stance is longer, you can step within the length of your stance as described above, which is preferable.

Static kick

In this method, derived from Thai boxing, you kick with little or no preparation. It's great at short to middle distances and can be augmented by a hop to extend its range. Many students find this much harder to do. The kick needs good balance and lots of practise to make it a stopper. Many people use this as a way of keeping the opponent away. However the best thing to do is to kick him in a sharp enough way to drop them, not push him away so that he gets another chance. Start from a short stance and make sure that your hips are up, so that the kick is half-way there. Raise the knee and push the kick forward. Let the hips roll under so that it adds power and you are more stable. After contact, withdraw the foot and the hips as fast as possible so that you can deliver further kicks with either leg. Snapping the kick in and out gives a more traumatic result.

Replace step

Sometimes you aren't in a position to get any power from the front kick without taking a step, yet you don't have the forward option open to you since your opponent is too close. Right: I've shown the replace step, where you take a short bouncing step backwards with your lead leg but without changing

Step past lead leg; kick

Static kick

Replace step

the direction that your body is facing. This builds a tension between leg and body, added to the power from the ground, to give you an effective and powerful kick. Like all kicks that have a preparation, it is easier to see and thus move away from. However, used in the right place it's very effective.

Round kicks

When I started Karate, I remember smirking slightly when the Japanese instructors called this the 'roundhouse' or 'round the house' kick, as that was their way of describing it. Once I'd been kicked in the head by one of the instructors a number of times I became much more respectful. As with the front kick, there are a number of ways of doing the round kick to make it functional. There isn't one single method that works well at all heights; different targets require differing approaches. Also, wearing shoes or kicking with bare feet can make a big difference to your choice of kick.

Low rear round kick to leg: Thai-style

The Thai-style low round kick is done to the outside of the leg, delivered from the rear leg. The target is about six inches above the knee. Kick, making contact with your shin, so that if your opponent moves closer you can knee him instead – and if he moves away you still hit with the instep. First, rotate

out the supporting foot as far as is possible so your toes point in the opposite direction to where you're facing. This rotation is vitally important. Bend the knee of the supporting leg so that you are kicking in a slightly downwards direction. (This kick can also be done horizontally and at a slightly upward angle.) Rotate the hips sharply to follow the foot and be careful not to move inwards and choke your kick up. Keep the leg straight if kicking a bag or kick shield but allow it to bend on contact if you are training with a partner, unless you want to do him some damage. Importantly, let the weight go into the kick so it has more bite. When practising, don't mistake speed for power and bite; emphasise heaviness and bite as you drop the kick in. You need to spend time on this.

Rear round kick to body

There are two ways of kicking to the body: one in a Thai style (similar to the kick to the leg, above) and the other with a snap approach and with the ball of the foot. Both are moderately effective, although if your opponent is in a left lead, both kicks will hurt, but rarely drop, him. I teach the Thai style first and then the other as a variation. Find out which works best for you.

Rear round kick to body: Thai-style

Just as with the low-line kick, rotate the supporting

Low rear round kick

Twist the foot

foot and allow the hips to follow; bring the hands across the body to cover and keep one hand tight to the face when the leg whips back. As before, keep the leg straight and hit horizontally or upwards. Concentrate on the basic kick and as you become more proficient you will work out the other variations, like turning the hip over just as you hit so it has more bite. Initially, concentrate on making it a heavy kick, with all your body behind it. This is a strange kick in that the more you interfere the less powerful the kick is. Emphasise the foot turn and the hip twist and let the leg swing free like a baseball bat. If you can feel the power in the leg then it's still in the leg. Heavy kicking feels effortless in the leg, though the body can tire.

Rear snap round kick to body: using ball of the foot

With shoes on this can be fairly effective as it goes into your opponent's body behind or under the elbow. Turn the hips over and raise the rear leg knee so that it blocks the direct line in towards you. This stops your opponent from coming directly forwards and prevents him from hitting you at the start of your kick. Extend the leg, hitting with the ball of the foot. Different levels of hip rotation will affect the reach of your kick – the more the rotation, the greater the extension – though too much twist makes it hard for you to recover and follow-up with hand blows.

Lead round kick to the middle

The Thai-style kick can be used to the middle but I find the snap kick more effective and harder for your opponent to grab. This is because the tool lands on his solar plexus, not the ribs which are under his arm where it's easy to grab and you can be thrown even if you get your kick in.

Use a pendulum or one-step covered by a hand strike or fake, or as part of a combination. Raise the leg at a 45° angle to block the centre line and snap the leg to full extension, hitting the solar plexus. Keep this kick short and it can easily be used with hands to make part of a constant barrage. Work on getting the ball of the foot to go into the holes in your opponent's guard.

Head kicking

Head kicking can be done using both snap and swing kicks. Swing kicks are very destructive and if done with good timing very hard to block – your opponent has to evade instead. However, it's best if you have a varied game. Snap kicks work best from the front leg whilst swing kicks work well from either leg. Snap kicks also work really well when done as part of a combo or after a low-line fake, like the one pictured here, where the attacker touches the leg with a fake round kick to the groin, then rotates the hips and snaps the kick to the head.

Lead round kick to the middle

Head kick from fake

The swing kick to the head is easier from the rear leg, but train it by doing it both right and left with either a stomp beginning or replace step (where you skip, switching leads, and use the bounce to power the kick) for the most ease. In actual combat, any method can be used.

Important: With snap kicks, point your knee at the target that you want to hit or a little bit further beyond so that you hit through the target. Remember to add your hips in as well. All kicks can change target half way through, though this is easiest with swing kicks.

Practise kicking high and then letting the kick drop like a swallow to hit the leg. Alternatively, start low and then raise yourself on your supporting leg to hit a higher target. The method for doing this is to first get the basic kick to all heights by doing lots of repetition. Then you know the shape of that entry. You can start with one type of shape, then vary the height of the kick as late in the motion as possible. Get your training partner to tell you if the fake looks authentic.

Side kick

It's interesting that different types of kick come in and out of fashion depending on what type of fighting is getting the most media coverage. At the moment, the side kick has gone slightly out of fashion but it's an essential part of your game. Favoured by Bruce Lee and others like Joe Lewis, it's also good in a self-defence mode. A friend of mine defended himself against four knife attackers in Morocco using a variety of kicks but most notably the side kick. His companion had his liver showing by the end of the fight whereas my friend wasn't harmed.

The side kick can be done from both the rear and lead leg, the latter probably being the most functional in one-on-one fighting. Here it is (bottom) from the lead leg with a faked high-line strike and a pendulum step.

To practise from the rear, it's important to load the kick properly. Bring the foot up in either of the two ways shown below. Twist the foot so that you hit with the edge. This isn't so important if you're wearing shoes but it still focuses the power more.

Foot position

Faked high line, one step lead leg side kick

Back kick

The back kick is one of those strong kicks which can be used when your opponent is very close or when you are spun off-line. It's hard to counter, whichever method you use. One method is to rotate and do a kick directly behind you without looking; it's sort of a reverse front kick. You ensure your accuracy by making sure the turn is right. Either step across and rotate or make your stance narrow like a side stance so that you can rotate and kick without preparation. The other method is where you rotate and look as you kick. This ensures that you are less surprised if he counters. It's sometimes called the spinning side kick as it shares a similar shape. I know from personal experience that this is hard to counter as it often curves inwards and can catch you on the liver even if you move quickly inwards to throw or hand counter. Try both ways as they both work: it's about having intent and belief.

It's necessary to build up the strength in the hips and make the muscles that support your balance stronger to make you a more formidable kicker. There are a number of training methods for this.

Slow kicking

You can just concentrate on slowing your kicks down when training with a partner, then do the final set fast. If doing snap kicks, don't extend to your full reach at speed as you are likely to injure your knee. Instead, take it to ninety percent and don't lock out. The essence of the kick is the knee raise and hip move and the snapback.

Obstacle practice

Kick, throwing your leg over a chair or other obstacle, or get a third person to kneel on all fours on the ground, whilst you and a partner kick slowly over them. Be sure to make it difficult for yourself by keeping close. When done slowly the hips have to be in the right place for you to hold your position.

Back kick

Obstacle practice

Hold outs

Firstly, extend your kick and hold it out as long as possible. Secondly, with snap kicks, you can hold your leg cocked and extend it at slow speed and bring it back, or hop down the dojo doing repeat kicks from the same leg without dropping it from the cocked position.

Tree exercise

Modelled after the Yoga 'tree' exercises, this works your balance and builds strength and core stability. Do this daily after a brief warm up and some simple single kicks. Do front, back and side kicks slowly but without putting the foot down. Once you can do this then add snap round kick to make it more difficult. For advanced students, try going from outside crush to front kick and then inside crush to kick.

Swinging your round kick

Thai-style round kicks can be done in the air. Go with the swing and turn your body normally, coming round and crushing with the opposite leg. Either repeat on one leg until you feel slightly dizzy, or alternate. Both types of kicks can be done over chairs or obstacles to build strength and the ability to put them where you want them to go.

Hold out

Knees

The knees are some of the best leg tools available to you. In a self-defence situation, no matter how closed down you are on the high level with little room to strike, there is always room to attack at low levels.

Long knee

This is a great technique to use against boxers. You keep your head at a less dangerous distance and attack your opponent's ribs as he attacks. Raise the knee and drive forwards in as horizontal direction as possible: think of driving a spear forwards. Failing to knee horizontally, instead lifting the knee upwards, makes you vulnerable to being spiked by your opponent's elbows and it's easier for him to block. At close range, you may have to tuck your body and raise and then roll your pelvis so that the knee still goes in a forward direction.

Short knee

This is the opposite of the long knee. Often used to counter tackles, the knee is raised quickly to hit the opponent in the head if he's dropped his guard.

Grab and knee

In conjunction with the head control, you can use a variety of knees. Use a simple direct knee driven forwards into the opponent's body – you can also go for the legs.

Training methods

Put your hands on your opponent's shoulders and trade long knees. Don't grab; just use the hand position to let you keep the same distance.

Lightly hand-wrestle at long guard then put in the long knee. Counter with a check to the chest or hip (right).

Long knee to the body

Checking positions; chest, inside hip, outside hip

Just as with footwork, if you want to be a good kicker you have to love to kick and make it a central part of your game. Work your close range boxing or clinch work as much as your kicks so that you don't have an area where you are weak. Your opponent will find out and attack your weak areas no matter how good your other tools are.

07: Simple Combinations

In this chapter we'll deal with learning and training simple combinations. Later, in Part 4, we'll move on to show more advanced combinations.

Combinations can be used both for proactive attack and reactively as a follow-up after a defensive move. Combinations also let you have an overlap in your distance. For instance, your front kick may fall short but the punch that follows it may go eighteen inches deeper toward your opponent. The following kick may then go a further metre. This overlap is important and keeps your opponent under constant pressure if he retreats.

Often when I am teaching I use the analogy of boxes. If your opponent was in the closest box to you (the punching box for instance) but now he's no longer there you know he's probably in the next box (the kicking box). This isn't fixed to punching or kicking but it should give you a better, more visual idea of distances. Sometimes your opponent's body may have moved into another box but his legs are left in place to be tackled or kicked, or the feet to be trapped.

There are three main ways to practise: on focus pads, solo training in the form of shadow-boxing, and training with your partner.

Focus pads

Good pad holding is essential. The holder can't be passive, but must direct the training, and should have a good knowledge of positioning and footwork himself. He can have themes which he works through when training you. There are simple ones, like checking your guard, and making you work your footwork. Then you can move on to defending against his mock attack and then doing your combination. Training can become even more interesting when he tries games, like trying to keep you in the corner, or moving you back and forwards or side to side to cut you off so you are trapped. Another way, as we will see, is when he attempts to tackle you and tries to take you to the ground.

How to hold the pads

The standard V position is good for most alternate blows. Notice that the angle isn't too sharp so that the puncher doesn't injure his wrist. For the jab and to check the guard whilst he does the jab, you can hold the pads in the L shape.

V position

L position

Holding the pads for a shovel hook

Holding the pads for right and left hooks

Holding the pads single for high kick

Holding the pads, single for low inside leg

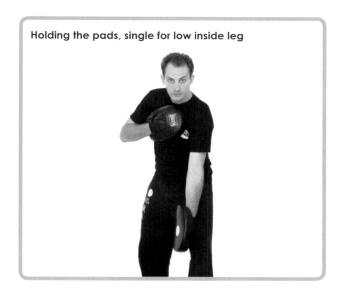

Holding the pads for uppercut

Holding the pads for light kicks

When holding the pads, remember that you need to give the striker some resistance. Push the pad slightly towards him on contact. It reduces the chances of receiving damage to your arm and shoulder from a heavy-hitter. Take the strain through the whole of your body so that you don't end up with injured shoulder and elbow joints like many professional instructors. Keep an eye on the angle of your pads and most importantly observe your opponent. This is a great time to watch his attack at close-quarter without being hit. Notice everything: how he prepares, how he moves afterwards and before, and log it into your computer. Work on strategies that will take advantage of his mistakes. Pretty soon this becomes habit and you will find yourself doing it with all your training partners, not only on focus pads but in your sparring as well.

Initially, do the combinations on the spot, just learning the moves. Then do them while moving your position between combos. This can be either as directed by your pad-holder or from one of the lists given in this book. This is where most students need to spend time: learning the mechanics and getting the combinations down with good form and power, then working on moving the feet between each combination.

After a while you can work in a more random way as directed by your pad holder. Interact with them; work on your measure, your power and on always having your feet in the right position so that you are waiting for your opponent, not the other way round.

Core essentials

These are the bedrock of your boxing technique. First, do these on the spot so that you get the hand and leg skills down. Concentrate here so that you can hear the right sound when you strike. Once you've got a resounding noise on the focus pad then you can start working through all the varieties of training that I have illustrated. It's really important to keep that tone throughout because it means that you're able to maintain your energy throughout a

fight. Don't leave the hand out there for too long but snap it back so that you can throw more blows.

Jab:

Jab as described on page 34.

Double jab

Make sure that you get your energy for the second punch from your ankles and legs and not from your arm. Punching from the top of your body or arm will mean that you telegraph the blow.

Jab – cross / straight right

Remember to hit by rotating the body. The head should move so it's not in the same place for both blows. Think about keeping the arms 'empty': if you can feel the power in them then that's where it is – it needs to be in your target. Keep blows snappy and relaxed with the hands clenched hard on contact. Line your body up so that you hit with the support of your bones.

Jab – cross – hook

Make sure that you rotate from the ankles and that you keep the elbow behind the hand for all blows. On the hook, the elbow should be at the same height as the punching hand on contact.

Cross – hook – cross

Don't prepare or wind-up for the cross; let your body follow your hand. Then use your ankles and legs to rotate between the blows. Performed in a continuous fashion, this is a good way to train the mechanics of your hook and turn it into a devastating close-quarter weapon.

Hook – cross – hook

Keep your wind-up to a minimum. If you have to do one, do it very tight and make sure you close your body in the process. You can sometimes lunge inwards on the first hook. Finish with the cross and hook.

Basic hand-leg combinations

Let's look at ways of joining simple strikes and kicks together. If you want to be a good stand-up fighter you've got to be able to execute simple links between techniques and be able to flow according to the distance and the opening. Most of the really good combative moves are the simple ones. Do lots of repetition so that it's coded into your muscles.

Jab – rear front kick

Open with the jab to get your opponent's attention directed to the upper quarters, or blind him to your real intention by aiming at his eye-line, then deliver the front kick.

Jab (off-line) – rear round kick

Jab at an angle, killing your opponent's jab response. Next, round kick his lead leg; that's where his weight is if he is jabbing.

Thai hook – rear round kick

Use a wide hook whilst keeping your body fairly square, to force the opponent to shift his weight to his lead leg. Then round kick it.

Tip: Timing

Once you've got used to striking on the beat then practise playing with the timing of the strikes by sometimes delaying one of the blows, usually the final one. If you pause in a sparring context, even though your opponent knows you are going to attack one of two targets, he has to choose. Once he gives away his choice you can hit the other target.

One-step front kick – jab – cross

Initially you should do this lead kick with a step, but you should train to be able to do it without. Don't fall inward as you front kick – keep your balance centred after the kick, then move forward with the jab and cross. The kick brings your opponent's guard down and you attack over the top. Remember to make the kick forceful and snappy, not a push, which only pushes your opponent out of distance of your punches.

Jab – cross – one-step front kick

Think about the box analogy when practising this combination. You try to hit the opponent with your first two hits but instead drive him back so that he moves into the next box and into the range of your one-step or lead front kick.

Jab – cross – rear round kick

If your opponent is slightly closer when you drive him back, then follow with the rear round kick to the leg he's left behind.

Front kick – round kick

A simple way of joining these two kicks together. Always do the first kick properly and with strong intent, not just as a preamble to the second kick. Pay attention to this in your training.

One-step front kick – round kick

A simple combo for longer range. You can always cover the one-step with a high line fake to lower the chances of being stop-hit. If you are in a shorter Thai stance and slightly closer then you can just kick without moving the rear leg.

Lead round kick – rear round kick

Here you can either use minimal footwork, Thai-style, if striking the lead leg, or do a pendulum step to snap kick the groin.

Lead round kick – cross – hook – cross

Use either the pendulum movement or Thai-style twist depending on the target. The pendulum brings the hands into play faster.

Jab – cross – hook – rear round kick

Here you overlap with the kick when the hand blows haven't connected with your opponent.

Five count: series one

These are great, simple combos known as five-count drills because there are five strikes or blows. They work on the simple body rotation that we'll practise later in rhythm drills. Not only are they great for building balance and integration but they also work every day when you have an opponent who retreats and you need to chase. Be careful about over-extending or putting your head in front of the attack. You can use either a lead front or round kick in these combinations and can also change the height of the initial kick. This makes it much harder for your opponent. In truth, combinations of more than two or three moves don't happen in sparring – or if they do it's with a break, pause or manipulation in the middle. What you end up doing is stringing lots of short ones together. However, at this level you need to build a base and extend your possibilities and the five counts do this wonderfully. Notice that the core of all of these is a simple body rotation starting with the cross-hook-cross and then just varying height, target and angle on subsequent variations. Later on you can preface the combos with different starting and finishing kicks.

Solo training

You should practise these combinations on the spot before integrating them into your shadow-boxing. Don't do too many; just choose from the list and make them yours one at a time. On other days do them all, one after the other. Once you've done them on the spot it's time to move. Choose a variety of footwork techniques and do them methodically, or alternatively just dance and jive around, feeling where your body wants to move. End your sessions without a plan; just playing, doing what comes naturally. Don't attempt to force anything. Put it in and let your body sort it out. Above all you have to go with your instincts. Play and joke around at times. Pretend to be hit and come back strong. Above all, even though you have to work hard at it, if it's not fun you won't do it. Relax and let your body do the thinking.

Training with a partner

All of the above simple combos can be done with a partner, in pair-work glove drills. These drills help you to learn to cover and move to the best position; when doing them, practise moving slightly off-line where appropriate. Don't lurch with big steps as this leaves your legs grounded and vulnerable to kicks; rather, keep on your toes. Later on I'll show the drills with a partner so that you get a clearer idea of how to use them. Though drilling in the air or on focus pads is good, there's nothing like working with a partner at a realistic range: you learn on the job.

That's all for the simple combos. Remember: combinations are important but don't overlook working the basics too. These are the ones that work all the time in combat.

Jab

Cross

Hook

Lead kick

Five count drills

1	2	3	4	5
Lead kick	Cross	Hook	Cross	Lead round kick
Lead kick	Cross	Body hook	Cross	Lead round kick
Lead kick	Cross	Uppercut	Cross	Lead round kick
Lead kick	Overhand	Uppercut	Overhand	Round kick
Lead kick	Overhand elbow	Horizonatal elbow	Overhand elbow	Knee – Lead round kick

In fighting you are at some time or other going to find yourself at close range. The head is one of the easiest parts of the body to grab so it's essential that you have some knowledge of head control and defence against head grabs. All of the head control and choke positions form a framework of positions that you can change between as the opponent's energy directs.

By working on the head and neck, you are attacking a vulnerable part of your opponent which affords good leverage. You can flow between the guillotine choke and the head and arm control with ease. Similarly, from the full clinch, half-clinch and side clinch, it is easy to flow into the head and arm control. Play gentle flow games, moving between these positions, or do gentle sparring using clinches in conjunction with elbows and knees. Play both sides of the conflict. As the saying goes about learning, it's important to 'see one, do one, and feel one.' Reflect this in your training. Remember not to depend too much on the knee and elbow at first, if you want to gain sensitivity and positional knowledge; however, later they should be used freely.

Half-clinch

Neck wrestling

This is basic neck wrestling as used in Thai boxing, a great place to start your standing grappling because of its integration of knee and elbow strikes. The neck wrestling puts you in a position to either use these strikes or defend more effectively against them.

Let's look at the head control clinch. There are a number of methods you can apply here but the one I prefer is to put both of your hands on the back of

Side clinch

Side clinch and knee

your opponent's head. Overlap the hands at the top of the head so you get good leverage and the opponent finds it hard to keep his head up. Keep your back convex – bent outwards – so that it's hard for your opponent to body-hold and back-bend you and take you down. Keep your elbows pointed into his upper chest and shoulders so you can use these two points to steer him. For both sides in this position, block a knee strike to the groin or higher by bringing your knee over to touch or cover his lead knee. The defender here attempts to bring his shoulders up to add support to the neck and makes sure that he has his body parts stacked directly under the head. If your hips aren't under you then you get pulled down to an easy kneeing position very easily. As a defender, you need to grab his back and pull him in, and do it quickly, as he will want to knee you and he needs the room to do it. In this way you neutralise his knee and can try to reverse the position.

To reverse the position, keep one hand on his back and insert your other arm between his arms till it's on his neck. Lever your elbow out whilst pulling in his waist: this lets you change his balance, open his grip, insert your hand between his arms and put it on the back of his head. Bring the other hand to join it and the positions have been reversed.

This just covers the basics of this position but it's a good place to start. It's important to keep the knee close to his leg and it's also crucial to keep your back in a convex shape so that he can't easily break your structure. Keep your head up and the head over the hips so that your back and hips support your head.

Head control, steering using the elbows

Block right hand blow to plumm

Block left hook to plumm

Ways into head control

There are a number of ways into the plumm or head control. Let's look at the simple ones which work well from guards and defences.

Use your long guard or shield block (p.82) to outwardly block a right hand blow from him. Lean slightly forwards and attach with the left arm and bring him into double head control. Start kneeing.

The rear is very similar. Block a left hook or slap from him and use the same blocking hand or your lead hand to attach to the head. It's a bit further from the backhand but still easy to do. If you plan to gain head control whatever happens then you're halfway there, because any mistake on his part means you've got his head.

From outside you can go directly for the head but sometimes the arm gets in the way. If this is the case, scoop the arm out of the way and gain head control. Sometimes he resists or his arm is stiff; when this happens, push it slightly first, then pull or scoop it and you'll be using his energy against him. Normally this is done in threes: you push or nudge him twice

and on the third beat pull or scoop him and he's working for you.

If you're unattached it's slightly more difficult and dangerous to grab the head. Again, it's important to plan to control the head so that when he's just finished attacking you can bridge the gap and grab.

Put your head down between your arms so it's less of a target, lean or lunge in, then attach and knee. This approach is very hard to defend against, except by creating distance very quickly.

When you do the rear parry against the jab, you can kill his rear hand with your extended lead and pull him in before he can re-apply the rear hand on a different line.

Head control doesn't only have to be applied defensively: it can be achieved when you do a left or right hook which goes too far or which your opponent bobs and weaves against. If your hand ends up behind his head then pull him in (to neutralise his boxing skills) and start kneeing or flow into other standing grappling. If the arm ends up on the side of his head you can either flow to a head-and-arm, or half, clinch or side clinch.

From outside to plumm

From unattached to plumm

In head control you often come up against a stronger opponent so it's important to have ways to deal with this. Make sure you are using your weight and not your arms to pull his head downwards. As he's stronger, attack his base with knees or body manipulation and keep him unbalanced so he can't bring his strength to bear. From the basic clinch, twist your foot round to the side. Keep your elbow in your opponent's shoulder. Twist his head slightly sideways to reduce his strength and then rotate body and head using the elbow as a pivot point. Your opponent will fly round to a new position. If you rotated your right leg then follow the twist with a knee with the left leg and vice versa.

Countering the plumm

There are a number of ways to counter the head control in a standing position.

> If you are being pulled about, try to keep your structure strong and attach to his back by clasping your hands behind him. If you can't attach, then use your arms to block easy knees and wait for one to come that you can deal with. (If the opponent is really good at kneeing the knee will come directly in and be more difficult to block or catch.) Scoop the attacking knee inwards with one arm and under-hook with the other. Drive your head forwards and up and push his head backwards whilst you lift the held leg. Step inwards a little and either sweep the ankle of the supporting leg or knee-bump his hips upwards (see picture below). Drop him to the floor and follow-up with strikes or, if he still has hold of your head, with a grappling follow-up.

Knee bump

Move to nullify knee attack

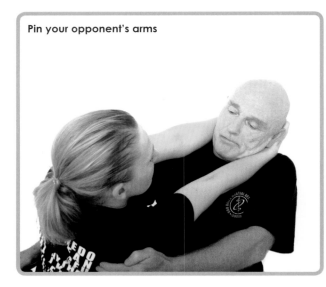

Pin your opponent's arms

> If he's not dragging your head around, you can nullify some knees just by moving in the same direction that the knee is coming. This often puts him off balance and you get a chance to reverse the position.

> Put both of your arms on his face with the palms overlapped and tighten your elbows so in effect it locks his arms up. Push, and his grip will normally break. Leave one hand covering his eyes whilst you start your counter-attack with a rear punch, and then kicks as he goes backwards.

> Whilst keeping one hand on his back, to keep you tied to him, push his elbow inwards with

your thumb. There's a point near the elbow which seems to work well for this. Then, once the elbow structure has collapsed, go forwards to jam his elbow against his body with your arm. Use this same arm to reach round and grab his neck. Place your fingers on the sensitive nerve points underneath his ear and swing him around. In essence his head should describe a semi-circle. Imagine that you have his head at nine o'clock. His head has to go through twelve o'clock and then around to three o'clock.

> A simple plan is to go with the energy and tackle his legs. You have to be careful as you are very

Face push to attack

Tackle

vulnerable to knee attacks so it's important to
have some sort of attachment to one leg as you
drop and tackle. The single leg tackle often works
best in this instance, though you have to go with
the flow. There are a variety of ways of tackling,
from foot pins to double leg attacks, which
you can add to your skillset as you progress.

> Sometimes you just raise your shoulders to
pin your opponent's arms, and use this pin to
swing him round. Generally, he either loses his
grip, or loses his position and balance, so you
can counter the grab or just counter-attack.

Elbow push in to head neck throw

09: Arm breaks & wrenches

Arm breaks and wrenches should play a significant part in your fighting armoury. To attack you or attach to you, your opponent has to use his arms. Therefore you have easy targets that he brings to you and that you don't have to go and look for. Of all those available, the elbow is one of the easiest joints to wrench and lock. It's less quick and less fluid than the wrist, for example: generally, the closer you go towards the body, the slower that part of the limb moves and the easier it is to lock. Let's look at building a repertoire of standing locks that work.

Outside / under

Use the shoulder or upper arm to wrench or break the arm. You can adapt this, if your opponent tries to escape, by moving his arm upwards to break it across your shoulder. This is one of the fastest ways to wrench or break and requires very little time or effort. It's important to roll inwards, bringing your shoulder behind his elbow. This is the best way to do the lock. The other way is to draw him in with your other hand, which works because often you'll have shoulder-rolled his cross. Other times he pushes: let him do the work. If he feels you pulling him then he'll pull out. Rather, guide him inwards.

Outside / middle

This is more of a drag-down or a pull-down. You can do it when his arm is straight but it often works better when the arm is a little bent. Rotate the arm

upwards (in a circular pattern if he is strong) and then pull down; it's very hard for him to be strong in a circle. Once you've broken his balance and he's facing floorwards, pull the arm away from the body and drag your opponent, spreading him out across the floor.

Outside / armpit armbar over / waki gatame

This is a very powerful arm break and hard to counter once it's begun, as all of your body weight is on his elbow joint. The best way to do this is to grab the wrist and strike at the head. The opponent always takes his head away to protect it but leaves the arm behind for you to break. Use the same punching hand to envelop the upper arm under your arm pit, pinching it with your arm so it's hard to get out. Put the hand of the same arm that's pinching on the opponent's thumb. Basically there are two ways of doing this: one where you walk through and give him a less severe landing, and the other where you pivot on the spot and stretch his arm out, whilst dropping the fulcrum (where your arm is pinching his upper arm) to the floor. It's as quick as turning on a light. Remember to not think about 'down' versus 'up' for the break; instead, think of elongating his arm and pulling or pointing it away from the body centre, whilst putting your ribs as a fulcrum down on the elbow. There are two types; circling, and walking through across his front.

Assisted arm bar with lapel grab

Here's a slightly harder variation to pull off, unless

Outside / under

Outside / middle

he's more compliant as a result of you hitting him. Do this if your opponent resists. Elbow him to the head then wrap his arm and grab your lapel or shoulder.

Arm lock flow

Overleaf I show a way of linking arm bars together in a very combative way. Often your opponent feels you trying to lock his arm and realizes it's going to get broken, so changes the axis on which you are breaking or moves his body. Here I start with an under-arm wrench but change it to a pull-down. Then as he changes the hinge axis of his arm and tries to bring the arm back closer to his body, I go with the flow and use his energy to put him in a figure four lock. For best effect make sure that you have your grasp at the wrist where it meets the hand, or slightly on the hand. This denies him any chance of countering the figure four. Should the figure four fail you can finish with an armpit armbar.

Outside armpit armbar

Under to middle to figure four flow arm lock flow

Inside wrap to wrench

The inside wrap is done when you use any of the
internal blocks like the shield or biceps stop. This
works against both the cross and the hook. It's
sometimes a good idea to wrap the arm with
yours firstly, to tie it up so you've killed one side of
his attack and can go into standing grappling.
An even better idea is to wrench the arm so it's
unusable. Then you've still got both arms free and
can continue striking, whereas he's fighting with one
fewer.

Head and arm control to break

Overleaf I show a way of breaking or wrenching
the arm from the outside, when you follow-up to
an outside parry, or sometimes as you under-hook
his arms as he goes to tackle you. If he tackles, his
arms are often out in front of him like the blades on
a fork-lift truck. Insert your arm as you elbow his head
and pivot out of his way. You then have a head and
arm position where you can redirect him into hard
objects or walls, or wrench his elbow. Normally if
his thumb is pointing downwards this is done with a
downwards double slap but if he turns his arm so the
thumb is horizontal then link the hands and twist the
body as if you were swinging a baseball bat and the
arm will break or be severely wrenched.

Inside wrap to wrench

Arm wrap to break

Two possible finishes

In Part Two we've looked at attacks using hand and leg tools, and we've seen how head control and arm breaks and wrenches can enhance your game. In Part Three we'll look at how to defend from these attacks.

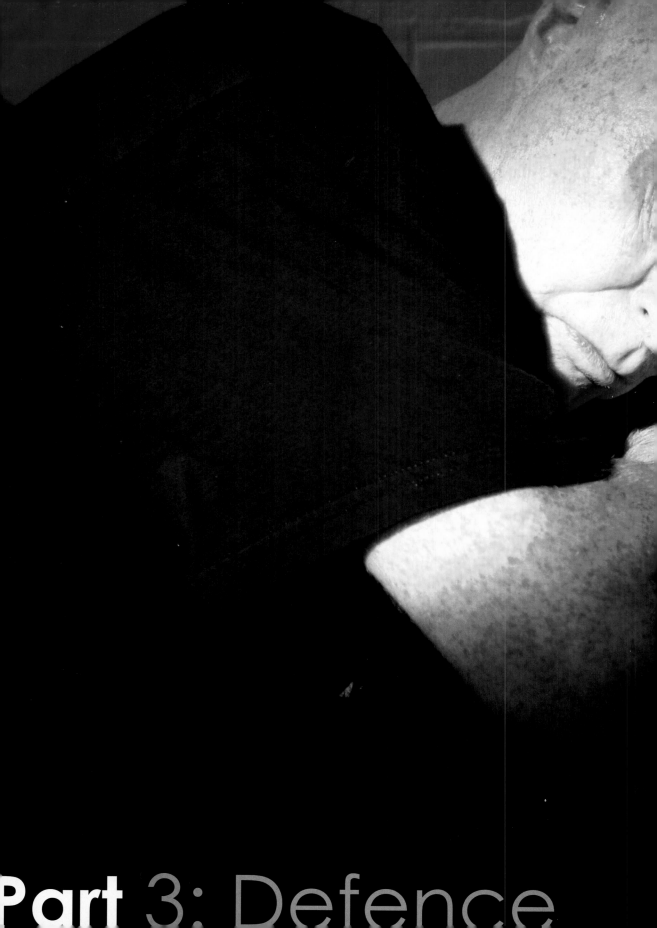

Part 3: Defence

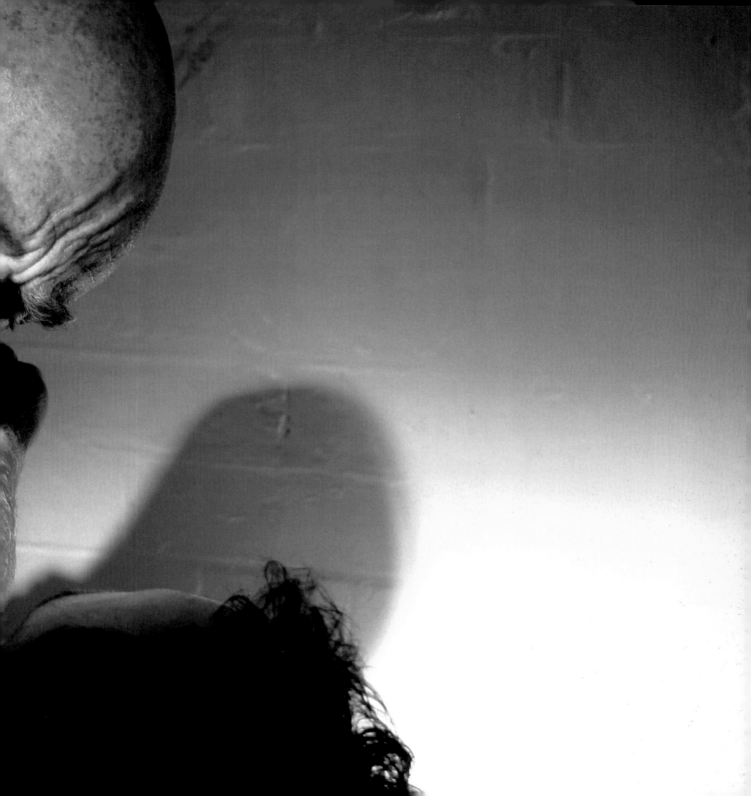

10: Punch defences

Having a great defence is the starting point to becoming a good or great fighter. You can get by, sometimes, if you only have an attacking style, but if you want to be able to talk about your successes in later years without sounding punch-drunk or showing lots of scars, defence is the place to start. Defence is your home, your fortress from which you venture forth to engage the enemy, or where you stay at home and counter-fight. Although we're talking about defence, let me restate that the best defence is still offensive in nature. Simply blocking blows might work in theory, but in reality what happens is that your opponent just tries harder, particularly if you block hard, which gives him energy to come back at you with. Each time you do a big blocking move, the opponent seems to get larger, whereas each time you hit him, he seems to decrease in size and power in quite a tangible way. Thus it pays to have a strong defence whilst always maintaining an attacking attitude. You can wait and take advantage of weaknesses in his defence or probe with attacks of your own to stop them, either before he gets started or to find open targets whilst the fight is underway.

Your defensive game comes down to only six options. These six can be mixed and matched and integrated with so many other finishes that there are too many possible combinations to learn one by one. Rather, learn the core skills, then have a small number of target finishes that you know really well. Improvise the rest based on sensitivity, intent and your experience.

The six basic defences are:

> Cover

> Crush

> Parry / scoop

> Stop-hit

> Grab or catch, and

> Evade

Initially, you will probably train these as they are taught either in this book or by your instructor. However, it's important to realise that you can radically change the basic technique by putting it somewhere else on the fighting time line (see Part 4). Sometimes it changes the whole character of the move. But that's what you want; simple skills that you own, that have so many uses that, were you to try to write them all down, it would be too complex.

Let's quickly look at the six forms of defence in the format I'd use for a new student learning to fight.

Cover

Covering is the first form of defence we teach to beginners. To cover, concentrate on keeping the hands up and the arms close to your body. It's all about learning how to ride a punch or kick and to curve your body so that it fits into the dimensions dictated by your arms. Thus, instead of moving the arm up and down to cover high and low blows and opening up other lines of attack, you just hunker down within your arm cover and learn to ride the blow using both body and legs to absorb some of the power. Covering needs very little timing skill, so it's the place to start if you've never been hit before. Start slowly and not too hard, if you are new to this. Aim to build up your toughness and durability over time.

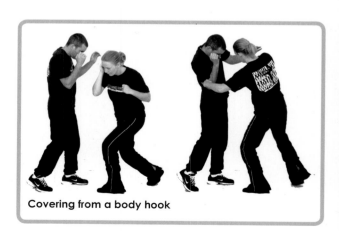

Covering from a body hook

Crush

The crush is one of the easiest forms of defence to learn and you don't have to have great timing to pull it off. Crushing is where you use your elbows, knees or shins as a defence against your opponent's blows. Filipino martial arts call this 'defanging the snake' and that's what it's like. You take the venom out of his blows by letting him strike these hard bits of your body. The resultant pain or breaking of bones deters them. Learning to crush is crucial if you are a novice fighter and need something that's going to work quickly. However, if you are dependent on crushing, it leads to bad footwork and evasion, so remember to practise your footwork.

Parries & blocks

Now let's move on to parrying or blocking blows. It's important to understand here that if you aren't going to counter-punch either during or after the parry then you are better off just moving out of distance or evading left or right.

Parries and blocks can be done at the start of the attack to jam or trap, but are used more often during, or towards the end of, the attack. If you are just starting out, make the parry or block first and then reply with an attack. This isn't the most efficient use of your time, but it is a good way for beginners to learn basic skills. Simultaneous blocking and hitting is more efficient than just passively parrying and then following up with a counter-punch. By blocking and hitting simultaneously, you gain a beat of time and it's harder for him to re-counter. It's important to have a good position with forward intent so that you are ready to counter-attack. A simple plan and aggressive intentions will make this an integral part of your game. In some cases you can use a block or parry after the blow or kick to cover the line so that he can't repeat his attack. It's actually very much like trapping. We'll go into more detail on the theme of parries later in this chapter when we look at jab and cross defences.

Stop-hit

The most time-efficient move is the 'stop-hit.' This takes the attacker out as he prepares or builds up power to attack you. This can be done with either hands or legs. Pre-emption nullifies your opponent's

Crushing a cross

Parrying a cross

attack before he gets going and is thus a great way to fight if you are light and facing a heavier opponent. You strike before he starts and then, if he recovers, you can evade until another opportunity to 'stop-hit' presents itself.

Grab / catch / immobilise

Then we have grabbing. This can mean catching a kick, or capturing or trapping the opponent's hand so that you restrict his body movement whilst you attack. Whether grabbing at the end of his blow's duration so that he is unable to retreat from your counter-attack, or keeping him off balance, there are lots of variations here, from simple grabs at the wrist, which are the most common, to close-quarter grappling where you close his options down. Grabs and traps work well in that they eliminate many of his evasive options and increase the number of hits you get on-target.

Evade

Evasion is one of the most difficult defences to learn and put into action. It needs a lot of work, therefore train it hard and often. Good evasion is the mark of the expert, so let that be you. Evasion can mean everything from running away, to foiling the opponent's attack with footwork, to simply moving your head so that the blow goes by you. What makes evasion so powerful is that missed strikes use up your opponent's energy. You can also strike whilst evading which uses your opponent's power against him. Most importantly, missing makes your opponent feel vulnerable and psychologically weaker. Evasion is quite possibly the most important and skilful form of defence, so let's cover its principles, and how to train them, in more detail.

Body evasion

Learning body evasion starts from a fixed base. Here we'll cover the standard ways of moving your body. Body evasion works better the closer you are to your opponent.

Stop-hit

Outside bob

Use your body's big muscle groups and move your head towards your opponent (see picture overleaf). You can accompany the bob with a punch to the body or head. Combatively, this is one of the best places to be, as it's hard for him to get you back. Sometimes, however, you can be vulnerable to chokes, so take precautions.

Bob/slip and simultaneous hit

Castle

Often when teaching defence to people I use the analogy of a castle to show them that relying on only one approach has many dangers. The important thing is to have defence in depth.

Let's look at the body as a castle. For hand attacks, the shoulders and the head can be thought of as the keep of the castle, the inner sanctum. Use the shoulder roll, the rear hand parry and simple head evasion to keep this area safe.

The next defensive battlements are the elbows. These can be used to crush the hands and feet of the attacker, as the legs can be used to crush low line kicks. Hands can be used as another line of defence, to parry either at the medium range, close to your body, or at long range using a long guard near the root of the opponent's attack. Use this to keep the opponent away or push his body off balance.

Lastly, the hands and legs can be thought of as aggressive patrols that go out and engage the enemy in his own land. If this defensive structure falls apart then you up sticks and move house using your footwork skills, then start again. This doesn't mean that you have to do all of this; just that you should see your defence as having depth, with each level or range of defence having a role to play.

During your training and when you are sparring, you should theme your defence around each of these components in turn to better know that skill. This isolation work pays dividends in your fighting when it's easy to achieve synergy by joining a number of simple skills together. This is much harder for an opponent to deal with.

Inside bob

Bob or slip his cross and reply with your own cross. If done against the jab, however, you can be vulnerable to his cross so you need to get close and 'eat his punch' or put your head in a position where you cancel out the mechanics of any blow. Sometimes you can even use your head to trap his rear hand whilst you move in.

Slipping

The meaning of the terms 'slipping' and 'bobbing' overlap; they are often used to describe the same thing. Don't worry about how you spell it; just make sure you know how to do it.

Slipping can be done with just a brief sideways bend, much like you may have seen boxers such as Mike Tyson do. If done incorrectly this uses small muscles and therefore it's tiring on your body, but it is very quick if you just want to get your head out of the way. A better way is to use the hips as a counter-weight. Throw the hips to one side and the head moves to the other. You can do this at a very low level of competence and as it uses the big muscles in the legs and hips it's not particularly tiring. Slipping doesn't close the distance but it does make your opponent miss, usually when he is closing the distance anyway.

Bob and weave

On the opposite page is a simple bob and weave against a left hook. You should repeat this against the right hook. When teaching this in classes we often start out with a fairly large movement: the student is urged to use his legs and think of his head disappearing down one hole and coming up another. As you get more skilled, the head leads the legs, but most students need to work all their body first and then refine it later. Though bobbing and weaving can be done reactively, when you have experience it's even better when done pro-actively, say at the end of an attack or combination. As with ducking and slipping, if you have a constant bounce in your knees these moves are always easy

Bobbing to the outside

Slip to the outside

to do quickly; the basic bounce simply needs to be amplified to become one or the other defence.

Duck

Change your level to make your opponent miss. Often best used as part of an attack where you fake high, to draw his counter, and then drop and come under.

Snapback

Make sure your stance is long. Bounce backwards on the rear foot; this enables you to return instantly to your start position – often with a counter-attack.

Bob and weave

It's important to use the rear foot to do all the work; only bend your back in an emergency. Think of your back as an airbag, flexing only if you do get hit. Don't move your lead foot backwards as this will permanently change your distance: instead, move the rear foot back about six inches and flex the ankle without letting the heel touch the ground. Snapback can also be done without moving the back leg; moving the back foot gives you about a metre in distance but you can still instantly bounce back to your original distance. If you don't move the back foot it's about half a metre. Simple drills like the jab-catch drill featured below focus on this element and produce good fundamental skill.

Vitally important in fighting at any range, the snapback is an essential part of your defensive armoury. If used in an 'attack by drawing' format you can make your opponent think he's falling short so that he over-extends. Then you can slip and counter easily, as he's done most of the distance change for you. This makes your strikes stronger as your opponent charges onto them. Alternatively, if his strikes drop short, the resultant 'hang time' leaves him open to counter-attack.

Snapback – jab catch drill

Training body evasion

Body evasion can be trained in numerous ways:

Partner

First, train statically against a partner's extended arm. Start with bobbing, then move on to slipping, then add bob and weave and finally duck. Do this rhythmically as a way of retaining it as muscle memory. Secondly, train against simple slow punches with a beat between them. Start with bobbing; add slipping and bobbing and weaving. Make sure you go at a slow pace to maximise the chances of success.

Moving in: Pulsing jab & extended jab entering

Use evasion to enter or get near to an opponent. These are two very similar drills I learned from my friend, Lance Lewis, who used to box out of the Kronk Gym in Chicago. Your partner walks towards you slowly, sending out a pulsing jab. You evade with whatever technique you like and try to move to behind his back. He adjusts and keeps slowly pulsing the jabs, moving to make it hard for you to achieve control over his back.

The 'extended jab entering' drill is the same but you keep your jab extended and in your partner's face as he attempts to slip, move and get your back. You adjust your footwork to keep him on the end of the jab. Use any method to get to his back as this will make you less orthodox. It's about body feel, and body knowledge. Both partners gain from this drill.

Pads

On the pads, firstly bob and weave, left and right, against wide single and double blows. Then hit the pads with simple hits, after which your opponent gives you large easy swings; bob and weave under these swings which get progressively tighter.

Then, to train at the next level, do single and double bob and weaves in both directions after you've hit the pads with single strikes and simple combos.

Lastly, you can pro-actively evade, where you double or single bob and weave after striking — whether there's a strike coming or not. You're taking the initiative and being a moving target. Come up to deliver more blows, or move to his back or to a safe distance using footwork.

Chair

In conjunction with parries you can do chair training, where the focus is on your upper body. Remember that the primary difficulty for your opponent is the change of distance and height. Moving long and then very close makes it difficult for him to hit you. Remember to go at a pace where you succeed and then build on that.

I remember training stick-fighting in a chair at home seven days after leaving hospital with my first hip replacement and beating the hell out of my training partners who never moved their upper bodies. They were so used to moving their feet, they were only using half of their potential. The secret with all evasion is to isolate the area you are working on and become good at that, then put it back into the mix. Find out the potential of every type of movement and make it part of your game.

Slipping drill

Here your training partner gives you a jab and then a cross, with a beat in between the two blows. Think of it as a rhythm of jab BEAT cross BEAT like that. If it's too fast initially you won't get the skill down. Slip the jab and jab to the body; return to your normal position; slip the cross and cross to the body.

If you hold your elbows slightly out from your body so that your arm has a dog-leg shape you will hit the solar plexus more often.

Bob and weave drill

Here you're learning simple bob and weave skills against slightly wider blows. Again, it's just a drill to learn the basics which you will adapt later to a more combative format. Your partner throws a wide slow cross, and you bob and weave under it, doing the minimum drop. Rotate your body from the feet,

letting the rear heel come up. Start with the left shoulder forwards and come up after the weave with the right shoulder forwards. You can minimise this later but for now do a big body rotation.

Let's take a look at the six counters in use against the main punches: jab, cross and hook. Train these defence techniques on the pads with a partner and in drills; you can then start to incorporate them into your arsenal to defend against actual punches.

Jab counters

Having a good jab defence is one of the key points of your defensive structure. There are three basic methods that I teach: the parry, the scoop and the catch. The principle for the first two is to let the blow go by, diverting it just enough so it doesn't hit you. In this way you can use your opponent's energy against him.

Let's look at these in detail.

Parry

Use just the fingers and the wrist of your rear hand to send the blow over your left shoulder. Make sure that you don't use a big movement from the arm, or take it to where you want it to go: this will leave you open to the hook. Just do enough to make it miss and then see if you can do even less. The parry can be accompanied by moving your head or slipping.

Scoop

The scoop takes the blow to the other side of your body. It's a great move for changing your opponent's balance and for opening him up. Sometimes it has the effect of asking him for the cross, so it's easier to time your cross counter this way than with the parry. Important: to make this effective you have to use snapback to create the room for his blow to deviate off-line.

Parry

Catch

Often used in boxing, the catch is easy to do. Just make sure to use snapback with it to cushion the force of your opponent's blow, as the punch will break through just a simple catch with the hand alone. Think of it as a brake on a vehicle that needs some distance to work. Used aggressively before his attack it can be seen as trapping. Alternatively, cling after the blow as he returns his hand, and trap to stymie any follow-up moves or to start your attack.

Training drill: isolation

In a sideways stance put your lead hand down or behind you. Now your training partner attacks with jabs at random intervals. Start fairly slowly and as you get better he can increase the tempo. By the end of a round of three minutes he should be throwing jabs fairly rapidly. You use only parry, scoop and catch to keep from being hit. Snapback is essential to take the pressure off. Use slipping to help you. Sometimes because of where your hand is you may have to do a salute-type parry. Keep movements small. Keep the lead shoulder raised and close to the parrying hand; this way you'll have less work to do.

Cross counters

The cross and straight right are two of the most powerful blows you're likely to get hit with, so it's important to have a good defence. If using the standard guard, keep it high and choose if you want to go into half guard. Don't just drift: be mindful.

Shoulder roll

Using the castle analogy, let's start with the keep. The shoulder roll can be used from either guard, and covers both wide and direct shots. Use the shoulder roll even when you use other leading hand parries, just in case the blow gets through. That way you've got a back-up, should your parry fail.

Scoop

Keep your chin tucked in and use the hand to catch the blow. Let the shoulder deviate the blow off-line. Important: Don't turn too much and make sure that at your maximum rearwards movement your body shape forms an equal triangle with the ground, not a rearwards triangle. This way you can still move your rear foot and retreat if need be.

Inside stop / shield

Against a wide blow, the stop or shield works well. The bicep stop and shoulder stop really work best if used pro-actively before he gets up a head of steam, whereas the shield can be used even

Shoulder roll from cross

Shield stop and bicep stop

Simultaneous parry, riposte

when he's at full power. Make sure that they are all supported with a raised shoulder, as you would with a shoulder roll, and by a good base from the feet. Variations from the shield are numerous and it's one of the best positions from which to gain control of his head or upset his balance, as shown.

Outside parry

The outside parry can be done in three basic ways:

Short parry

Initially it's used short, just to support an outside slip to make sure that the cross isn't going to come into your line of evasion. Follow with a strike.

Simultaneous parry, riposte

Alternatively, parry and at the same time reply or riposte with your counter. Remember that doing this while he is attacking is the best method. Another method is to use the closest tool, your parrying hand, to do a 'half-beat strike' which either chops or backfists the opponent in the face in the time between your parry and your big follow-up. Done this way he often doesn't see the big hit coming.

Long guard

Keeping the parry long is one of its most effective uses; using it from a long open guard invites him in, thus allowing you to attack by drawing. In this method you close him down and thumb him in the eye if need be. Keep the elbow down and hand open. The long guard should have a forward energy whilst also closing down the opponent. Make sure to close at your centre, rather than only out where the hand is. Think of it like a contra-flow on a motorway. He is coming towards you on the same side, but you are making him move over to the other side of the road whilst you stay on this side. Rotate the hips slightly and push with the back leg.

Scoop

The scoop is used to drag the opponent in a little, to put him off balance before scooping the hand in a clockwise direction, using your body and back foot as the power source for this. Sometimes you can attempt to close your opponent down with your long guard and then when he reacts you use his energy to make it easier to scoop. If done properly his head pops out like a tortoise's and he is easy to hit. Once you've scooped, you can use your scooping hand to either control the head or to do a bicep or shoulder stop, to stop a follow-up blow. Alternatively, mask his face with your hand so that he can't see your follow-up blow.

Elbow crush

Here I've shown four possible ways of using the elbow crush.

Keep the hands high. From a long or high guard, fold your face into the crook of your elbow. Sometimes you can lean back slightly, to make sure that the attack lands on the point of your elbow. If blows are landing on your arms then you either have to fold further inwards or use snapback to make it land on the important part. It's important to remember, with the elbow crush, that if you can see your opponent really well, he can hit you. Learn to do the crush so that only one of your eyes can see your opponent. Alternatively, for the instant that he connects, cover your eyes with the elbow so that you can't see. However, don't let fear hold you there; it's just for an instant. The best method, as I say, is to hold the elbow with one eye only able to see his body. If you're using vertical elbows against hard blows make sure that your hand is anchored on your head. Move forward and use the elbow crush much like a carapace or shell that allows you to go forwards under fire and attack his castle. Always threaten your opponent's position or balance.

The elbow crushes can be used together in combination, sometimes doubling them up. In particular, from the diagonal and horizontal crush you can move to a grab or control with ease. Once you've got both elbows up, it's for all purposes the same position as the cross guard. Mix this in with your

Horizontal

Vertial

half-guard and long guard and you have a great defensive structure.

Active cross counters

Split entry

In the split entry you cover with an outside parry whilst thrusting a strike into the gap between his two arms. This can be a spearhand to the throat, as shown here, or it can be a punch to either the head or body. Often if you scoop the preceding jab then you influence the timing of the cross and know when it's coming. In addition to striking high, you can strike to the solar plexus. The opponent's turning and forward energy only adds to your punch; you use his energy against him. As with the slipping drill, make sure you have your arm a bit bent in a dogleg shape so that you connect with the plexus easier.

Hook counters

The hook comes from outside your range of vision so it's important to have a good guard from the start. If jabbing, remember to cover with your rear hand on the diagonal so that you can cover both the jab and the hook easily. The rear hand is normally open so that it's able to catch defensively whilst remaining live and able to hit. Don't just keep it clenched, passively covering your jaw, as you won't use it to hit and it says a lot about your fighting psychology. If you think defensively it gives an experienced fighter lots of clues as to your mindset.

Cover

It's important to know how to twist the body so that your cover works more effectively. Just a slight rotation makes it much safer and means that your cover defends more of your body.

Stop

The stop is applied to the hook the same way as the cross, and similarly can be used to stop a blow at its inception. This works best after scooping the hand out. Then you cling, keeping in touch with your opponent's hand, and stop him at the bicep or shoulder, then follow-up with either a cross (if you're twisted a little) or a hook (if you're twisted a lot). You can also do the stop to defend from the jab, but this needs more skill than a parry as it's harder to maintain close contact as he changes to the hook.

Shield

Just like the shield against the cross, the shield against the hook needs a low level of timing skill and

Split entry

Stop to the hook

Shield from the hook

is great for either attacking the arm by wrapping, or as a lead-in to throwing or head control. It's good for moving into the plumm or head control, and also for moving into the arm wrench.

Simultaneous cover and hit

This is a more active way of defending against the hook. Cover with the hand held palm-forwards in a shield position, which is the strongest defence, and strike with a vertical punch which needs less room than a palm-down punch. Then continue with follow-up combinations to finish your opponent.

Bob and weave

Bobbing and weaving is a great way to evade the hook. To make the bob and weave more workable make sure that it's happening in a controlled way all the time, meaning that the knees are always bending and the head is moving slightly all the time. This way you just have to amplify what you are already doing on a micro level to have a fully functional bob and weave. Bobbing and weaving should be pro-active, not reactive in nature. Bob and weave even if you don't need to. This is like moving your castle just as your opponent is planning his attack. The only way you are going to ensure that you will have it when you need it will be if you are doing it all the time. Learn to love to move.

Crush

The elbow crush can be used in three ways against the hook: to the hand, to the biceps and to the chest. This normally depends on how deep your opponent attacks but you can also choose where you want to crush.

Simultaneous cover and hit

Crush on hand

Crush on bicep

Crush to chest to silat take down

11: Kick defences

Kicks are powerful, long-range attacks. If used by your opponent in conjunction with hand attacks, kicks can draw your hands or legs to one area or line, whilst you are being attacked at another point where you are less prepared. It's important to recognise that sometimes good kickers are good at kicks because they are weak at closer ranges and have developed their kicks to keep people away. It's your job to challenge this. As I said in Chapter 6, if your opponent knows his basics well and is really good at kicking, he is going to be harder to counter and you may find it very hard to get close enough to check out his close range skills or to counter-kick. A good knowledge of defence will give you a much better chance to do this.

A sound knowledge of the basic skills and ways to train them is important, as is the importance of having a simple plan. First you should understand your guard and stance. Next you should focus on blocking methods. This means not doing any movement too large, keeping things close and tight and with good alignment, so that, in closing one area, you don't open another and expose your centre line or major targets.

As we saw with punch defences, there are only six basic defensive things that you can do against any attack. Once again they are:

> Evade
> Crush
> Parry or scoop
> Stop-hit or stop-kick
> Grab or catch, and
> Cover

You can do these singly or in combination.

Let's take each type of kicking attack in turn and look at a range of suitable defences to them.

Front kick

You can use four of the six ways of defending against the front kick. Passive covering doesn't work because the kick penetrates your centre line so directly.

Of all the major kicks the front kick is the hardest to defend skilfully against. It's easy and direct, and fast for your opponent to do. It doesn't place him in too much danger and there is little preparation if he has his hips raised.

Skills developed against this kick will have benefits in terms of courage, timing and position against all the other kicks.

Evasion

Evasion techniques against the front kick largely fall into two categories. The first type of evasion is moving to make his blow miss, and instantly or simultaneously counter-attacking. The second is when you move to simply get out of the way and then choose whether to leave it at that or to reply with your own counter-move. Obviously the first is more active and more offensive in nature and uses fewer beats of time. The second gives the kicker more time or more beats to recover and to possibly counter your counter. If your footwork is good then the second type of evasion happens without a thought, so it's the first, offensive, type that we should concentrate on.

An effective defence is one where the same techniques work against as many blows or strikes as possible. Have a small number of skills that you know well, and then adapt them with distance, timing and placement to fit the circumstances. Notice as we go through this chapter how many of the counters are very similar and just have to be adapted slightly for differing attacks.

Body evasion and rear punch

This is an advanced technique which takes quite a bit of courage and intent. You use attack by drawing and lure your opponent in by offering a juicy target. Simply twist your hips and side step a little as you twist. Don't do too much, as the intention is to be close enough so you can deliver your punch rapidly. Most people worry too much about the incoming kick, evade too much and it doesn't work. Let it scrape by you. Do the math and see that the only part of his kick that's dangerous is the point, where the foot is. Evade this and you're hitting him with his own power *and* yours. Warning: be careful of follow-up punches or fake kicks as this technique will leave your head open. Be prepared to slip and counter-punch. This can be done without a supporting outside scooping parry or with it. Practise it without at first then add the parry if needed.

Body evasion, rear punch

Body evasion; enter and lead punch

This is most effective against a lead kick, but if it's used early enough it works against a front kick from either leg. Step in and twist so that you evade the kick. Foot placement and timing are important here. If you hedge your bets and side step too much then you will be too far away and the kick will get you. Step directly in. The preparatory part of his kick, when he lifts his knee, is the time to move. Step directly and then twist to evade the kick whilst punching. Support your counter-attack if needed with a low block which just deviates the kick. Don't try to block it, but move it marginally off-line. This counter can be done against both kicks but is harder and requires better timing and more courage against the rear. However, timing and courage are good attributes to acquire!

Body evasion, lead punch

Evade and groin-kick

This is so simple that many people don't ever use it. There are two ways of doing it. In the first, you are going to kick with your lead leg, regardless of which leg your opponent kicks with. Simply step with the rear leg either way, depending on the kick, then rotate your body out of the way and kick to the groin with your instep. In the second method, move your leg to the side and kick with the other leg. Both methods work with amazing ease. If you really want to drop him then this has to be in your armoury.

Retreat and counter-attack

Evading by retreating works fine most of the time but if your opponent attacks deeply then you can find yourself overrun. Therefore I recommend the more aggressive counters. If your opponent thinks you're going to punch him in the face, he attacks with less vigour. A mix of drawing him by retreating and counter-punching works great. In this example you retreat by moving your stance as a whole to the rear, then counter-kick with a rear front kick. His kick stretches too far and either has 'hang time' or drops forwards to the floor leaving him open to the counter-kick.

For all the other passive evasion use the footwork patterns that we covered in chapter 3. Don't be heavy on your feet and have a bounce in your knees. Move early so that you don't have to react at the last moment. Use footwork to draw the opponent in, to stretch his blow just that little bit further, in the hope of getting you. Then use one of the aggressive counters.

Crush

The crush is very simple and can be used passively by just raising your leg and closing your guard so there are no holes. Alternatively, you can just raise your leg and skip inwards towards your opponent, jamming his attack, then finish with hands or hands and legs. It's important in both of these to have forward momentum.

Evade and groin kick

Retreat and counter-attack

Crush

Parry

There are a number of parries that you can use against the front kick. Let's go through the safest and easiest to do, then onto the ones that require a better sense of timing or which carry greater risks.

Scoop parry

Use this against a kick from either leg of your opponent, though it's best if you use the one on the opposite side to his kick: if he kicks with the left you use your left hand to scoop. It means his body is closed and it's less easy for him to follow with another kick or hand attack. If you do it the other way, it still works but you enhance your opponent's ability to follow with a round kick. Make sure that you move the arm in a circular fashion so that you don't jam your fingers and that you come from below the kick. Important: In pair training and shadow boxing make sure that you instantly bring the hand back up to the high line. Your opponent could be faking you low, to draw your hand down. There are two scoop methods:

Scoop and throw

Scoop the ankle of the kicking leg and throw your opponent's leg as you move your own body. Kick the leg as it lands on the ground because at this point the weight is transferred to it. You can also throw the leg in the air and attack his supporting leg, which has the weight on it.

Scoop and retain

Tuck your body and scoop the leg upwards, and initially towards you, to overstretch him. Then, move it back towards the opponent, attacking his balance. When his balance Is broken, attack his standing leg.

Elbow deflection

The elbow deflection is easy to do but highly effective. Just push your elbow forwards into his kick, whilst slightly curving or tucking the body, so that the kick goes by. It can be done using both elbows, though a deflection against a lead kick has a higher

Scoop and retain

Scoop and throw

chance of success. Like the scoop, this is best if you deflect him so that it closes his body and the only follow-up is a back kick or spinning hand attack, which has to come a longer route. Follow-up with hand, leg, or grappling attacks. Important: use the minimum of movement. Don't go too far off-line but try to keep your hand tools pointing at him. Keep hands high to protect against spinning hand attacks if you close in.

Outside parry

The outside parry is great as it really turns your opponent. Use it with the earlier evasion to guarantee you don't get hit. The weakness of this is that you leave yourself open to a hand follow-up as your lead hand is low. Only do this when you see the opponent is fully committed or when your intuition tells you it's the right thing to do. Move your head out of the way as soon as the parry has changed the path of the kick and hit with your rear hand. Don't linger too long with the block or you'll get hit. Alternatively, you can scoop the ankle at longer range and just lift the leg to once again threaten his balance or throw the leg to open up his body for your counter. Follow up with a rear stomping throw.

Elbow deflection

Outside parry to punch and rear stomping throw

Low block

Combatively, the low block is not the best block to do: your hands are low, dealing with the kick, and the top of your body is open to attack. However, like all things it's about how, when and where you do it. Everything works in the right place. Whilst it can be used in a basic parry and counter-attack format, this will only get you a short way before you are being faked low and hit high repeatedly. Psychologically a hard block gives your opponent positive feedback and he tries harder. If used to support jamming counter-punches, it works great. Use it as a way in to grab and throw, as shown in the next chapter.

Low block

Grabbing / catching

Because the front kick is a direct kick, the catches that work well are the ones where you are going to go on and throw. Use a low block, supporting a high level attack to keep your opponent distracted. In reality this is a stop-hit, a parry and a grab combined. From here if you are close enough you can do the bump takedown against the knee.

Bump takedown

Lead punch counter to inside reap takedown

Folded leg

Oblique

Side kick

The low-line sidekick is highly effective for your opponent to do both in attack and defence, and difficult to counter. Let's go through its counters.

Fold

Fold your leg back either a small amount if your opponent's kick is aimed low at the shin or swing it more from the hip if it's aimed at the knee.

Meanwhile continue with an attack or entering strategy on the high line. This way he only gets one chance to kick.

Fold and re-kick

If your body is more side-on, you can retreat your leg until his leg drops at the end of the kick. Sidekick to his knee.

Raise and re-counter

Alternatively withdraw, raise your leg and front kick. Use this as the beginning of an attacking combination.

Oblique

The oblique to the groin works against all lead side kicks at low and middle height.

Mid and high level side kicks

The counters to the front kick can be used against the mid-line sidekick because they share the same line. This is what you want: a simple fighting plan that covers all eventualities. The sidekick occasionally angles in under your lead elbow so you have to be accurate in your counters. Also the sidekick is the opponent's longest kick so his body is further away. Any entry that you do has to make allowances for this. Some of the counters shown now are the same as those for the front kick.

Elbow deflection

Just as you did before, tuck your body and push the elbow forwards to deflect the blow. If you feel the elbow won't do the job, instantly switch to the scoop which will work fine.

Elbow drop

Here you tempt the opponent to kick, by keeping your arm slightly raised, then drop the elbow. Change your body axis by leaning slightly forwards and drop your body weight so that your opponent's kick is spiked on your elbow. Don't use the arm; use the body drop instead. You don't do much, but what you do is highly effective.

Elbow deflect

Elbow drop

Drop palm

Snap your body back a bit and, as in the picture (right), change the body angle for a moment so that you use your body weight to parry the kick. Drop the palm or the forearm on his sidekick. Think of drawing it slightly backwards towards you. Don't look down but keep your eye contact on his chest or eyes. The best follow-up here is one where you use the same arm to finger jab high, either to hit or to fake, so you can groin kick low. Then you're off and moving.

Double pillar

If it's thrown at the right distance, your defences against the lead high side kick are very limited. This is one of the few times a cover will work.

You'll either have to move backwards using this or alternatively use it in a jamming motion. Standing where you are often just gives you whiplash as the kick hits your arms and upper body.

Crush

The sidekick is weak at its start so it's a great kick to jam. Just raise your leg and hop inwards, with your hand weapons poised for action (see picture overleaf).

Drop palm

Double pillar

Crush

Evade and scoop to rear groin kick

Evade and parry combination

Evade and side kick

Here you evade to the left and kick to his supporting leg with your side kick. If it's done to your right then evade and rear groin kick. Though these are good defences, you need to be athletic if you attempt this without a supporting block or parry. Use it in conjunction with a low block or parry like the scoop and you have more time and are on to a winning formula. Just use the scooping block to throw the leg to the side and then, depending on how much you've turned your opponent, move in with hands, legs or grappling.

Evade and scoop to spearhand groin kick combo

If you want to keep your skill set to a minimum for maximum combat effectiveness just evade and groin kick as before.

Stop-hit

Sometimes you can see the preparation for a lead side kick quite early so it's a great opportunity to just stop-hit your opponent.

Stop-hitting strategies

You can use your legs to stop-hit against all attacks. Let's look at some methods; the one you use is determined by where you balance is, how much time you have available and what feels the easiest to do.

First is the front kick. You can stop-kick with either of your legs very effectively. If you are too slow or late in starting then the fastest option is to front shin-kick. Swing your hips and raise the instep so that you don't jam your toes. Alternatively, raise your leg to begin a kick but turn this shape into a leg crush. It's all based on how much time you have available.

The next one to have in your toolbox is the lead side-kick to the low line. This works best when you're side on. Just hack away at the leading leg either as a stop-kick counter or as a disturbing attack. The line between the two is blurred if you are pro-active. Alternatively, lift your leg high and side stomp kick to the knee, if you have the time. If that doesn't work, adapt it to a raised leg jamming technique and hop in and close with your opponent.

Finally, there's the oblique kick. The oblique can be used to the shin, knee, groin and stomach as it arcs upwards. Where you strike again depends on how much time and space you have.

Round kick

The round kick is a very common attack. It's easy to throw and easy to block. Let's go through the progression of defences that we use at my Academy. This really works and gives you a safe and effective means of learning. Once you've got some of the basics down you can start using variations which require a better sense of timing and are faster.

Cover

Move away from the kick. Important: keep your balance neutral. Don't fold over towards the kick, or turn your back, offering him the three target jackpot of two kidneys and a spine. Rather, curve your body into the size of your arm. Think of curving the ribs closer together by lifting the hips and curving the back so that the ribs are more like one, and less easy to break.

Cover and scoop: basic

Here, you move and cover but use the furthest hand to pin the opponent's foot against your arm. Then use this furthest hand to scoop and throw the leg. You angle and attack the leg just as the leg lands on the floor. Once you've got this down and your timing is better you can just do the scoop on its own.

Cover and scoop variation

Here you throw the leg in the air and attack the rear supporting leg where the weight is.

Cover and near hand scoop

You can still retain the foot against your arm if you need to. This is useful for students who don't yet have the timing perfected. Then use the nearest hand the hand of the arm you're covering with to scoop and throw the leg to the side.

Cover and under-hook

Do the same as with the cover and near hand scoop. If you've got good timing then under-hook the kick as soon as it hits your protective cover. If you need more time or reassurance then use the furthest hand to retain it for a moment till you can do the move. It's all about making the opponent fit to you, about you not being in a hurry or getting flustered. Let him have the problem, not you.

Double block to under-hook throw

Use the double block as another way into the under-hook. By following this method, you'll make it hard for him to kick you in the head. Keep the low arm slightly bent so it acts as a brake or speed bump to

Cover and scoop

Cover and near hand scoop

a high line kick. Check the thigh with your lead arm and under-hook. Twist your body so that you are the maximum distance from his punch, then step in and inside reap his supporting leg. Make sure that you turn in the direction he is kicking – it's much harder for him to counter and the throw is much harder. Then either finish with a groin punch and turnover or attack the knee using either a lying knee bar or a standing knee wrench. For best effect, step in and twist so that you are throwing in the same direction as the kick and be sure to reap the standing leg into the air. See p.100 for pictures.

Over-hook to reaping throw to Boston crab

In this example, as soon as you've over-hooked, punch him in the head with your rear hand and stop his forwards motion. Then step through and reap his leg. Keep your back straight so that you aren't pulled down and your opponent doesn't end up half-twisted. Just continue by stepping in the direction he is twisted. Keep your back straight and apply the leg lock, or use in combination with a hip/back stretching lock.

Lying knee bar with two possible finishes

Boston crab

Over- and under-hook strategy

Let's look at when to over-hook and when to under-hook.

1. If you're extended, OVER-HOOK

This means that if your opponent kicks you as you are punching him, close the ribs and absorb as much of the power by moving in the direction of the kick, and over-hook the leg. Make sure to use the blade of the forearm to pressure the shin as this makes it harder for him to do a number of counters. As this isn't the strongest way of holding, you are vulnerable to your opponent counter-kneeing or closing to plumm head control.

2. If you're not extended, DOUBLE BLOCK TO UNDER-HOOK

This is a stronger position and you successfully block your opponent's attack. You are, however, vulnerable to a jumping knee, triangle choke or arm bar. Make sure to check his nearest shoulder and twist your body so that you are the furthest distance possible from his punching hand. This stretch also sets up any following throw you might execute, so it's essential to do.

Obviously if in sparring you find yourself doing one when it would, in theory, be better to do the other, don't worry: just continue doing what comes naturally. Theory is smooth, whereas reality is rough. There is no absolute way of doing things that guarantees success. If something's working, go with the flow and don't get in your own way by being too analytical. Afterwards, if you like, you can analyse and maybe train the other method more so it's a more instinctive part of your technique toolbox. Above all, it's about instinct and intention; using what happens and going with it.

Over-hook

Double block to under-hook

Crush

When you're learning the crush, it's important that you don't build bad habits which can lead to simple counters. There are two primary ways to crush. Firstly, block with the portion of bone just below the knee, where the head of the shin bone is. This is the least painful method. However, to get that part to hit every time needs lots of practise.

The other method is where you turn your leg out so that it's at a sharp angle to your body. Any kick landing on it meets your shin with your thigh bone pointing outwards, which means the force of the kick is met head on. If possible, block with the part of the leg below the knee, but it's not essential. If you don't turn the leg out enough, your crush will often fold against a strong kick.

The crush can be used for all kicks up to the mid level. Tie it in with the arms and a curve of your body and you have a good defence. If you constantly lift your crush high, the opponent can fake the kick high and then drop it to attack your supporting leg. If you lift it, keep it quick and only go as high as needed.

Note: the crush is painful to do. You can condition your shins by hitting Thai pads and hard bags. For training, wear shin pads to protect. In real situations it's probably a one-off pain. Never show him that it hurts you. Keep your eyes strong.

Crush to same leg kick

Crush the attack and then step to the right and kick with the same leg.

Crush and standing leg kick

Here you crush and then re-kick with your standing leg. Use the force of stomping the crushing leg down to add power to the kick.

Crush to lead leg kick

Use a lead leg crush. Don't drop the leg but engage the hips strongly and front kick with the same leg. This

Crush to same leg kick

will disrupt your opponent's balance. Follow up with a right round kick.

Cross crush to rear round kick

The cross crush can be used if your weight distribution is wrong and you can't easily crush with the nearest leg. You can use it with follow-up round kicks or on its own as a destructive defence as shown below. Ensure you keep strong eye contact with the opponent so that you show him that it didn't hurt you – even if it did! It's all about breaking his spirit.

Cross crush

Evade

Evade and cut kick

Evade with a triangle step and round kick to the supporting leg of the kicker. Sometimes called a cut kick, this is best if it angles slightly downwards so it breaks the stability of the supporting leg. Bend your supporting leg to make it its most effective. It can also be used in a slightly upwards direction if you are short of time. Enter strongly. In training, be careful to not overdo this with your training partner as repeated blows to the back of the knee can aggravate this sensitive area.

Evade and side kick

Evade and side kick

The 'evade and side kick' is harder to do than the cut kick but even more effective as it goes across the knee structure. The difficulty is in making accurate contact as you have a smaller target area than the round kick. This needs to be practised diligently to have the greatest effect. Be careful of your training partner's knee by kicking with control.

Cut kick

Time line

On this page is a time line of sorts, showing your opponent's attack at various stages and some counters that could be used at each stage. This isn't a rigid time line: you can both attack and defend at any point along it in a variety of ways. However, it is a useful idea to hold in your head whilst training.

Early stages of attack

Lead leg low and high line kick

The only trouble with these kicks is that they don't look flash; they just do the job. Get these working and then play with your more flashy kicks once the opponent is more fearful and under your control. Alternatively, mix with high line kicks to stretch your opponent's defence. As you can see I've only outlined a few kicks, but because they are easy to remember and to use they are more likely to work, and you will gain confidence.

Lead hand stop-hit

Later stage of attack

Very late stage of attack

Catch over and under

Double block

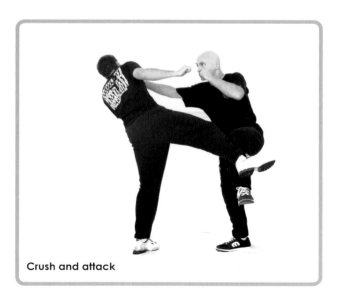

Crush and attack

Under-hook

Training methods

Drill all counters against single slow attacks first. This is the place to do lots of reps and put them into your reflex patterns. Then practise using simple combinations so that though it starts differently you learn to see the shape of the attack you're working on, even when mixed up with other attacks. Then practise either in an alternate kick-for-kick pattern where you each take turns, or with one person feeding alternate legs. Start by having a basic cover that you are confident with, then mix the other options in. Occasionally scoop, then change to working on evasion and cut kicks, and then finish with crushing. If you haven't got the time or the skill down then go slower or cover to give you time to think. Once you've got that down, work the stop-hits in. Crushing is the easiest to learn and to do, so if you need to be up and fighting quickly then that's the way to go. However, if you only focus on this quick fix, which works fine with pads on, your footwork and evasion and parrying will suffer and when you haven't got pads you may be at a disadvantage. Ring the changes in your training program so that you don't become dependent on any one way. Remember: always have a strong yet flexible stance, with all your tools pointing at the opponent and keep strong eye contact. The only way he knows what is going on in your mind is by what you show on your face. Don't show him anything. Alternatively play with him by appearing agitated when you aren't and calm when you're not. Be the puppet master. A large percentage of fighting success is dependent on psychological aspects. Become the master of this by doing it and looking confident in all drills. Strong eyes!

Time management: If you have lots of time, work your counters both sides to keep you flexible and to have a balanced body structure. If you have time work the weak side even more. Most people don't, but if you do, you're coming at your opponent from a side he isn't used to. It's all about how much time you have. If you haven't got much time, keep it simple and just concentrate on mastering one side.

12: Throws

Throws are a great way to defeat an opponent. An opponent may feel defeated just by being put on the ground. However, be aware that throws that don't disable an opponent often have to be concluded with a finishing technique, so that the opponent is no longer active. Only then can you take care of any further opponents. Throws differ from style to style and system to system depending on what they are designed to achieve and the culture from which they come. Some are big, dynamic throws where often you land on top of your opponent and continue the fight – if he's not already disabled from the power of the throw – by grappling and ground striking. Other types of throw are more like body disposal: you have dealt with the opponent by striking him a number of times and the throw is a way of putting him on the floor in what is, for you, a strategically strong location, often in the way of other opponents. Once you understand this difference, you will understand the uses to which you can put each throw.

Counters to the jab

In this chapter we are going to start looking at throws from the standpoint of the techniques and basic positions that we have already covered. Let's start from the slip against the jab. This is one of the most common defences and also one of the least risky.

Body tackle series

Slip the jab and go deep so your head is near his armpit. Alternatively, your opponent's attack is such that you are already quite deep. Grip your opponent's waist as shown and pull in tightly so that he gasps. Don't be too nice: your aim is to fold him in the middle. You can do this in two ways. Firstly, dynamically use your forward momentum. Push your head to the left and take him down whilst bending his body in half. The other way takes longer but is surer. Grasp the waist, keeping stable with your hips low and near his, and push your hips forward so that his legs are off the floor. Dump him to the rear.

For both methods, if the throw doesn't seem to be working, trip with your right leg. If this isn't enough, often you can step over and land on your opponent in a mounted position.

Punch and body grasp

Leg tackle series

Slip and parry the jab, then drop down (with your guard up) and tackle your opponent at the waist. If the body tackle isn't working, or the position isn't strong enough to throw him, go lower – and use your sensitivity skills to recognise early on if it isn't working. Remember that attacking the opponent at one of the three key points – the top, the bottom and at the hips where the body hinges – is the main concept.

You can drop and attack the legs in a variety of ways, firstly by a single leg tackle. Hold the leg tightly; you can hold it just above and behind the knee and near the ankle. Keep his leg as straight as possible. Step forwards with your right leg and then, using your head as an extra lever, twist towards the left. This stops your opponent using a sprawling defence. Take him to the floor.

Secondly, use a double leg tackle (pictured overleaf). There are two ways to do the double.

You can dynamically attach to the lead leg whilst threading your other hand behind the rear leg and driving forwards. Alternatively, drop from the body tackle position and pull both your opponent's knees together, with your hands clasped behind him. Step forwards and lift his legs as you twist to the left and dump him to the floor. Done properly, this tackle can be controlled and slow for training purposes.

Thirdly, do a foot pin and throw. You can either continue as shown for the other two or perform a rolling leg break which brings you on top of your opponent, ready to strike.

Learning the basic concepts will make your leg tackling much easier. On the street, the leg tackles have to be modified, as dropping too hard onto concrete can injure you as much as your opponent. Good conditioning will make all tackles easier to do, and in particular will make you less averse to changing levels so that in turn you become harder to tackle yourself.

Single leg tackle

Double leg tackle

Variation: foot pin

Leg lock

Counters to the round kick

If you kick, your balance is compromised as you only have one leg on the floor. Here I show ways to counter the swing round kick. This is the easiest kick to catch and throw from, particularly if the attacking leg lingers.

Inner reaping against a kick

Catch under

To start this drill, either cover and under-hook, or use the double block to check his kick and then under-hook as you did against the round kick (p.105).

Catch over

When you catch over, it is important to lift his leg by rising up on your toes. Once you're up on your toes, push back towards him. Take control of his body. Make sure that the hard edge of your arm is biting into his leg so that he is unable to bend his leg to knee you, or come closer so that he can strike you. You are the striker: take control.

Head and arm windmill throw

This throw, also known as puta kapala, uses the weakness of the head and the leverage of the arm to throw the opponent to the ground. When you have achieved head and arm control in some way, and have moved to the side to avoid a tackle attempt, knee him, elbow him then use the throw to dispose of his body in a way which is strategically sound for you. The alternative method is to use your elbow to slow your opponent's forward motion. Attach and throw, moving back so that he can't attach in turn.

There are two ways to throw your opponent with the greatest ease. From the side control, line your opponent's body up first so that he is easy to throw. Secondly, if you attach properly you can use the momentum from this attempted strike, redirecting your opponent's forward energy to throw him. Concentrate on the striking if you are on the side and have the head and arm position. Concentrate on redirecting if you are directly in front of him and he is coming towards you, as you have less time to play with.

Unskilled tackles

Often in real fighting the tackle attempt is just a need on your opponent's part to get closer and to stop you hitting him. He will often turn his head

Head and arm windmill throw

away whilst reaching out with his hands. Many times his eyes will be closed or averted. Take advantage of this to introduce him to a hard object if you are street fighting. In the dojo, playfully redirect him towards the wall so that you get to practise thinking in this manner. Don't slam him into the wall but simulate this; it goes without saying that it's important at all times to take care of your training partners.

Once you've thrown your opponent you can finish him in a number of ways. You can stomp on his head, with an arm break to finish. You can alternatively stomp and finish with a lying arm break. I've also shown how to counter if he manages to grab your leg using an octopus head wrench. Go to the right if he grasps your left leg and to the left if he grasps the right. Be careful when doing this that you are applying all of your body's force against one of the most sensitive parts of his body: his neck. For this reason, when training go very slowly, and take lots of care of your partner.

Unskilled tackle…

…re-direct and introduce to hard object

Octopus head wrench finish

Head lock throws

The basic front headlock works well. It tends to cause pain but doesn't affect your opponent's consciousness, like a rear choke, so as a result it's a place to be prepared to move from. Because it's painful, you get a range of reactions from your opponent which you can use to help to throw him to the ground.

Guillotine...

Throw

Stomp finish

Guillotine to stocks

Rolling head lock

Head and arm

Rear throws

Attacking the rear is safer for you as your opponent's limbs don't work particularly well there. Therefore, attacking the back gives you a huge strategic advantage. Watch out for rear head butts, low groin strikes and spinning elbows plus rolling leg locks. Although these require vigilance, they are about all you have to watch for by way of easy and fast counters to the rear position.

Ways to the back

There are a number of ways of gaining control of your opponent's back. Here I've just tagged them onto some of the basic skills that we've already covered, so you don't have to learn new skills but just go a step further with the ones that you know already.

Slipping the jab

Slip the jab and either punch or body tackle. Pivot on your leading leg and rotate the rear leg behind your opponent. To keep him from rotating the same way as you, check his rear or furthest hip. Working on the nerve there disrupts his balance. It doesn't work for everyone but is usually highly effective and you aren't fixed there waiting for him to counter. When moving to the rear, raise your head (as shown in the crucifix drill on p.116) so that you don't get guillotine choked. You can slip and attack the rear on the cross but it's much more difficult and leaves you vulnerable to the knee if he's facing you. Use this only when he is off-line and you can see the opportunity.

Kick scoops

We saw the two methods to scoop kicks - one using the nearest hand, one the furthest - on page 98. When using the nearest hand, step to the rear as you will have only moved him off-line. Then stomp and choke using one arm to encircle the neck and the other to facilitate the choke and to add power.

In the second method, drag your opponent down, then pin him against your leg and push your thumb into the neck notch. Attack the nerve there whilst you rip the face, and hammerfist attack.

When using the furthest hand, enter and if the head isn't available, as it often isn't, grab the waist and take him down to the floor to finish him there. You can use the bump takedown, where you pitch him up in the air on your hips and then, when his feet are off the floor, drop him to the floor. Alternatively, drop to one knee and use your forearm against his hip bone to drag that hip to the rear, and to the ground.

Slip and hip check to get the back

The best thing about scooping kicks is that it instantly gives you your opponent's back. Be careful in moving in as it's very common to get knocked out by a spinning blow. Keep your hands high until your head is on his back. Keep your head down to avoid getting hit by rear head butts.

Arm drags

You can move to the back easily by arm-dragging your opponent. Your opponent throws a wide blow; you stop it and, with the furthest hand, under-hook with your arm and drag him, so that you are at his rear, or at least part way. Then repeat on the other side. You can also do this from wrist wrestling or other clinch positions.

Crucifix drill

Your opponent hold his arms out in a sort of crucifix pattern and you step under his arm with the leg on that side, dropping as you go under and then looking upwards towards the ceiling. Make sure that your hips are underneath your head so that your body shape is strong. Then repeat on the other side.

Arm drag

Arm drag

Crucifix drill

Clavicle drag

Part 4: Putting it all

together

13: Advanced combinations

In chapter 7 we looked at some of the fundamental combinations of strikes. In this chapter I'll introduce more ways to make the most of these in defence, and also introduce combinations for use at closer range.

Long range

You can increase the usefulness of the simple combinations we looked at earlier by putting one of the five types of defence in front of them. If you're doing the five count drills in training, you sometimes have to add another strike or kick, or conversely subtract one, to get to your starting position. However, you will find pretty soon that you just flow naturally and fill the gaps. Remember that the six types of defence that you can do are: cover, stop-hit; crush; evade; parry; grab (or clinch). Some of the combination elements are given as a refresher on the following page, but refer back to the relevant earlier sections of the book for full details.

Opponent attacks with a cross or feigns a cross

You defend with:

> Stop-hit with lead front kick to body. Finish with rest of five count

> Crush – horizontal hammer which acts as the first blow of the combination. Continue with the other four blows of the five count

> Outside parry before his punch from a long guard – eye gouge as first count of combination and continue with rest of five count

> Outside parry during his punch – right cross to body as beat two of combination and finish five count with hook – cross – lead round kick

> Evade with bob and weave – hook – cross – round kick

> Inside bicep stop – five count or cross – hook – cross

> Inside shield – arm wrap or wrench – five count

> Bong sau parry – arm wrench. Finish the rest of the five count

Crush

Hammerfist

Inside shield

Lead front kick stop kick

Lead round kick

Crush

Evade, cut kick

Evade and grab

Cover and scoop

Jab

Cross

Hook

Uppercut

Shovel hook

Stop to bicep

Opponent attacks with a round kick

> Stop kick to stomach – five count

> Stop kick with oblique kick to groin – round kick to groin as the starting kick of the five count

> Crush – round kick to his standing leg and then finish the five count

> Evade with cut kick – five count

> Evade and grab – cut kick – knee and leg throw away – combination

> Cover and scoop – throw away – simple combination

Opponent attacks with a lead round kick

> Crush with lead leg – five count

> Stop-hit with lead punch as first move of four/five count

> Evade by retracting your lead leg (toy gerk) and reply using a lead kick from the withdrawn leg. Finish the four/five count

This gives you a number of ideas of how to fit the five count or other combinations into your training. Focus on one initial defence and get that response down by doing lots of repetitions. Then, if possible, do it for as many attacks as possible. For instance, the stop kick and stop-hit can be done in the same way for almost every attack. Similarly, the crush (using both the arm and the leg) is very easy and doesn't require expert timing. However, because the crush is so easy (though sometimes painful) make sure that you work evasion first, and just as much as crushing.

Though here I've only shown how to use the four or five count, you could do lots of different types of combinations or partial five counts. For instance, just do the cross and round kick from the five count, or the cross and hook. Also, see how you can fit in the other combinations shown in chapter 7.

Tip: Focus on one thing

If training any combination, spend a long time on just one attack and get that down, then put it back into your list. Work out where the preparation is on your attack and learn to hide it.

Medium and close range

At medium and close range you get more chance to use the uppercut and shovel hook. Many students attempt to use these too early and don't develop a good enough jab and cross. Work on those first, then when your opponents are consistently getting past them, it's time to work on shorter-range tools.

Here I've shown the use of combinations which integrate the use of the uppercut, moving from long range into medium range.

> Jab – lead hook – rear uppercut – hook

> Jab – lead hook – step with rear body hook and high hook

> Lead shovel hook – rear shovel hook – tight or wide hook (Use when you are head to head with your opponent and he has a tight guard. Slip to the inside and shovel hook, then slip the other way and finish with a hook.)

> Lead uppercut – cross – high hook (slip to the inside and uppercut up the middle. Finish with a cross and high hook.)

> Rear uppercut – lead uppercut – right cross low – high hook

> Rear uppercut – lead uppercut – overhand

> Rear uppercut – lead hook – cross

> Lead uppercut – rear uppercut – tight or wide hook

> Lead uppercut – rear body hook – rear high hook

Close-quarter combinations

Just as with the trapping entries into combinations (p. 125), you can start your counter-attack or combination from close-quarter positions. Start from the half guard position where you find yourself once you have slipped or bobbed to a position close to your opponent's armpit. Alternatively, use this approach when your jab has missed and your opponent has slipped to that position. What often happens is that in this loose, untied, clinch position you both re-group and have a rest of sorts.

Keep your back leg strong, as often it makes him think that you are backed up against ropes or the wall and have no backwards options. Then, when you choose, you can just snap-back to a slightly longer range, giving room for your tools to work.

From the half guard:

> Bump him to make the minimum of space, just enough to get your punch through. Rear uppercut to lead hook. Follow with cross – body hook – cross, or go back to clinching where you can't be hit

> Snap-back instead of bumping and repeat the combination above

> Elbow lift: Snap your elbow upwards quickly to bring his head up from its hiding place

near your armpit, then cross – body or head hook and cross or rear elbow – lead elbow – rear elbow and knee

> Kidney slap: Pivot on your lead foot so you're no longer directly in front of him, and slap to the kidney area to bring his head up. Go into cross – body hook – cross or any other applicable combination

> Bump, using your horizontal arm to bar his options, and hook to the head (make sure to keep the hook very tight so it just goes around his guard). Follow with appropriate uppercut or cross-led combinations

> Lead elbow pick up: Using the hand from either on top or underneath, open his body up and right hook to the body, with the hand down and the lead knuckles biting. Repeat the right hook to the head and continue as targets present themselves

> Rear pick up: Pick his elbow up with your rear hand whilst stepping in and pivoting to the left. Follow-up with lead body or head hooks and then continue with combinations as you see fit

Bump

Elbow lift

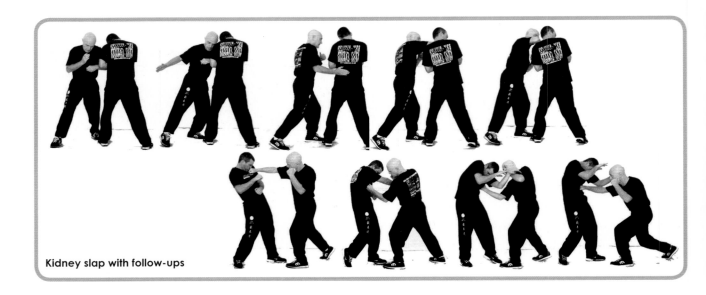

Kidney slap with follow-ups

Lead elbow pick-up

Training combinations: partner

Combination work is intended to build your ability to flow when you are fighting, so it's important to keep this in mind when working with an opponent. Both of you should wear bag gloves, as these small gloves make you work your technical skills better than a larger 12 or 14oz glove. There are three main ways of working here – in fixed combinations, defensively and pro-actively.

Fixed combinations

Start with your fixed combinations. You attack your opponent with the agreed combination and he parries, covers, or evades as defence. Regardless of your level, there is work of this type for you to do here: firstly, to maintain your existing skill; secondly, to explore new combinations, new ways of attacking. In sparring, the training partners with whom you spar will eventually get to know your game, so your game has to develop. The way to do this is through repping new combinations or approaches.

Defensively

After practising the above, do the same combinations after blocking or parrying a defined blow which your training partner throws at you, much as we did on the focus pads. He attacks you with a cross, for example, and you block or parry and then go into your combination counter-attack. More advanced fighters can practise their combinations against any one of a group of defined blows. It means you are just tagging the combo onto the end of a parry or block.

Important: Cut down the time between the defence and the counter-attack when doing this sort of training. Almost see the parry (or slip or block) as the first count of the combo. You should be on your toes and moving forwards or at least having a forwards intent when doing this sort of work. This makes you pro-active even in your defence.

Pro-actively

Finally you should do combinations pro-actively, which works really well in sparring. This is where you ask a question: for instance, you throw a jab – which often elicits the same or similar response from your opponent – then you parry or evade and do your combo. By fighting this way, you develop a good idea of what his response will be, as opponents often respond with the same thing you've thrown and this puts you ahead on the timing. This is complicated if you want to do a back-and-forward training drill with your partner. Here are a few of my favourites which work really well in sparring. Train them with your partner, giving the response you want and then practise in slow sparring so you find where it works. By doing things pro-actively you steal time from your opponent.

> Cross – salute

> Jab – catch

> Jab – cross – failed hook – bong sau – follow-up

Take note: you can't do these in a backward and forward style as easily as the simpler combinations. Decide how many you are going to do and get him to attack you in the way you want. Learn the shape and you can make up your own combos. Research

Tip: Don't telegraph

Get your body position right so that you don't have to do a wind-up or a preparation, because the necessary tension is already there within your stance or position. This is much like an athlete on his marks at a race: good position will cut down any dead time at the beginning of your attack.

what happens to you in sparring so that you can be ahead of the game.

Trapping to combinations

Simple traps, where you trap your opponent's attack against him, work well as a route to combinations, whereas more complex traps depend on sensitivity and lots of training. Simply trap the first hand barrier that he presents and then finish with a combination. There are three ways of doing this. As I have said before you can do these on your own, with a partner, or on the pads. Here we'll show them with a partner as this is where it works best.

Stop the jab (overleaf)

This is just a light touch on his lead hand. It stops the countdown and he has to go back to his mental start line, or hook you, or hit you with his rear hand. It's simple and effective.

> Jab – cross – hook. Bounce the hand from in front of his jab to stop his countdown then go directly into your combination

> Bong sau / rolling arm defence (against the cross) – cross – hook – cross. He strikes with the cross as soon as you trap his jab. You defend with your lead arm and then strike back

> Stop on jab, then slap and follow with cross – hook and round kick

Stop the jab, then jab cross hook, alternatively bong sau

Single slap trap / pak sao, to:

> Cross – wide hook or slap – rear low round kick

> Cross – hook – cross – lead round kick

> Cross – round kick – round kick

Grab / lop sao, to:

> Cross – body hook – head hook

> Cross – round kick – rear round kick

Three-for-three

One of my favourite exercises to do with a partner
is three-for-three or four-for-four. This is very simple:
you throw any three-count combination at your
opponent and he responds with any three-count
that comes to his mind. This makes you mentally
sharp and also teaches you how to cover. You have
to have a body of knowledge first, but once you
have that then you are off and moving.

Start with the standard combos. You should work at
making them penetrate the holes in your opponent's
guard. Once you've got three or so of these down,
you can change between them at random, so that
even though your opponent knows broadly what
you are going to do he still has to be able to read
what is going to happen. If you find this level easy (I

Pak sao

Lop sao

don't) then you can go on to being more random in your attacks, as long as they are within certain boundaries. The aim, after all, is to build on success, not only for you but for your training partner who is practising defence. Aim at holes in his guard and interrogate his defences. You don't have to repeat just the standard combos. These are useful for teaching you the basic patterns, but you can break the patterns by changing target, repeating blows and hitting where he's open. Probe his defence and think out of the ordinary.

If you have problems and are getting hit a lot when you're attacked, then go back a step. Go slower and refine your defence and cover.

Four corners

This is a way of integrating the combinations that you know with a simple defensive cover. Depending on

the range, use either the first or second combination listed.

In this drill the pad holder tests your defence with a hook or slap. You then respond with the following:

> Against high left hook: cover with tight cover and respond with hook – cross – hook, or, if closer lead uppercut – rear uppercut – hook – cross

> Against high right hook: cover with tight cover or shield and then respond with cross – hook – cross, or, if closer, rear uppercut – lead uppercut and cross

> Against left body punch, body hook or slap: cover with elbow then respond with left uppercut – right uppercut – hook

> From right body punch: cover with elbow and then respond with left or right uppercut (depending on where you are) – cross – hook

High right hook

High left hook

Left body punch

Right body punch

Start slow but ask your training partner to increase the speed of his attack so that it happens at the end of your combination and there's less of a pause between moves. If the skill level gets worse or disintegrates, then go back to a slower pace. Any combination can be used using hands, hands and legs, knees or elbows. Use your imagination but drill the basics.

When you are defending, keep your feet pointing at your opponent as much as possible. Don't over-react to his attacks. Point your body towards your opponent to ensure your energy is focused in the right direction.

Tackle attempt combinations

When your opponent attempts a leg tackle you can use these four simple ways to counter, to be used alongside your striking. If you do this on your own in shadow-boxing, use your imagination but make sure you move enough, and correctly. If done with a partner I find the best method is to practise on the focus pads.

To simulate a tackle, the pad holder does one of the following:

> Touches the floor, or

> Charges with hands behind back, or

> Charges with head down and both hands extended (also known as a bear hug attempt)

Sprawl

The pad holder touches the floor to signify that he is making a tackle attempt. You sprawl, which should put you on top of his body with the ability to choke or reposition so that you control his back. Make sure you keep your head up. Get back up quickly and punch.

Pivot

The attacker can come in for a tackle attempt in one of two ways: with his arms out, which allows you to wrench, or with his pads held behind him and his head exposed. Pivot out of the way, either on your lead foot or by withdrawing your lead foot, and perform the redirect on the other side. This is very similar to what a matador does with a bull. Just move out of the way and perform the follow-up combination.

Tip: mix ranges

Work long range combos in with flurries of close range strikes and then move out, making sure you don't retreat in a straight line. Go back to using your jab or straight kicks to 'stick and move' again.

Pivot

Sprawl

Head and arm

Use the same footwork as the pivot, but pick up the opponent's head and arm, with the arm in a potential arm lock, and redirect the head – in a real fight towards any hard object. Counter-attack with a knee and then finish with the combination.

Short knee to combination or cross and round kick

Use a short knee to stall your opponent's tackle or to bring his head up, followed by a standard combination or one sided combination.

Arm wrench or throw to combo

When applying the arm wrench, use the same body mechanics as if you were doing a right or left hook and then finish with the rest of the combination.

As you can see, just adding these simple tackle defences to the combinations that you already have gives you a formidable defence.

Combinations with a head control or clinch ending

In these combinations we will focus on either doing a full head control (sometimes called the plumm) with knee attacks, or a side head control (often called the side clinch) again with knee attacks. With the full head control, remember that, rather than bringing the knees straight up, you should drive them in so that they are hard to block. Once you can do standard knees you can vary the type of knee attack and also change heights, much like we did in the three-for-three and four-for-four training earlier in this chapter.

Tip: hand position

When putting your hands on top of your opponent's head, remember to overlap the hands (don't intertwine the fingers) with the elbows grasping the head tightly. It allows you to direct his head easily to the left or right, or hold it in one place.

With the side head control, make sure that the elbow is down inside your opponent's shoulder, if he is close enough. The hands should be overlapped again, with slight spiral energy towards the top of his head which makes it harder for him to oppose your energy and counter the position. For the sake of space we will just focus on the attachment and ending. You can add any of the previous combos that will take you to this reference point.

Lead front kick – jab – cross – side clinch

Jab and cross and, as your opponent slips to the outside, pivot and control his head. Double knee and then either deliver a straight shin to the head or push away and round kick to his legs.

Lead round kick – cross – hook – head control / plumm

If the hook goes wide and your opponent's head is within the circle created by your arm, pull him in and give three knees to the stomach, then push away and kick. Alternatively, switch to half-head control to counter his tackle or grapple attempt. Finish with a combo as above, or a hand combination.

Side clinch

Jab – cross – hook – side clinch

Sometimes your hook misses and your opponent has the opportunity to come in behind it. As on the tackle attempt series, pull back the side under attack, pivot as you retreat and pull him into side clinch. Knee and follow-up as before or just finish with a choke. If the choke fails, you can finish with one of your favourite combinations.

Kick grab counter – plumm

Here your opponent grabs your round kick. You crash in and push the leg downwards whilst controlling the head strongly. Follow this up with knees then with a combination, low round kick or tackle / single leg pick-up.

Kick grab counter – plumm with knees – leg pick up – knee ride

Grab his kick and punch to the face or focus pad, then gain the plumm position by whatever means you like. Drive in the knees if your opponent's energy is backwards and upwards (he's trying to lift his head), then let go and perform the single leg pick up. Take him down and throw the leg to one side. Knee ride and strike the face area or focus pads if he has them.

Tip: making music

Your body learns best when all of its senses are working for you. It's important to learn with rhythm and sound as some of your key helpers. If doing combos first, learn them on the beat with the emphasis on good body mechanics. Get your shoulders moving and your head. Once you've got the beat then break the beat or play with it. If working on focus pads or Thai pads concentrate on the noise that the strike or kick makes. In the start, work on making this a resounding and sharp bang on all blows of the combination. Don't go further till you've got this.

Key points

You should first learn combinations on the beat with the emphasis on good body mechanics. Get your shoulders and your head moving. If you're practising with an opponent, don't rush in. This is a common mistake: keep your body behind the punches or kicks so that you don't telegraph. This is one of the hardest things to practise: when your training partner backs up too much, as they often do in a drill, you find yourself chasing him with your head in front and raised. Be careful, cautious and aware when doing partner work. Remember that lots of quality work can be done on your own; you don't need to coordinate with a partner so it can be done any time, anywhere. Instead of wasting those spare moments, do your combination training and see the results after just a short while. Let's look at ways of doing all this on your own, which is a great training method.

Training combinations: solo

In solo training, as in all training, you get to build muscle memory through repetition.

On the spot

First, start by just going through the combinations that you've outlined, on the spot. Don't do too many different types at one workout; to build muscle memory you have to repeat things over and over. Five different combinations in a workout should do for most students; you can add more depending on how much time you have.

Footwork-based

Next, do the same combinations but with simple footwork drills. For instance, curve left, do the combination, curve right, repeat the combination. This can be done with almost all the footwork drills we've previously shown. Slide and step doesn't work so well with this format as it primarily works on into real fighting. When you have some experience you should go back to your shadow-boxing and add what you have learned to the format. Have forward intent at all times, even when moving back. Don't stand still; be a constantly moving target. See yourself as a winner at all times.

Breaking the mould

Finally, break the combinations by only doing them in a partial format. For instance, only strike two and three of a four-count combination and add this to your shadow-boxing, or any two numbers that fit together well. Do this while at the same time concentrating on body mechanics, balance and body feel. Change the rhythm of the combinations, sometimes on the beat, sometimes missing a beat. Keep a bounce in the knees and change your body height to mix the height of your blows. Similarly, work both long distance and close work. Make your combinations and your footwork like a dance; enjoy moving through your body.

a forward to backwards axis, but practise using this great footwork to break in and out, use it during the combination to break ground, and try putting the combination at either end of it. This sort of training can be seen as footwork training, but if you link footwork and solid combinations you are onto a winning formula. Make sure that you don't fizzle out at the end of your combination and die on your feet. Keep your feet active and use a jab to get you out of distance so that you can start once more on training your routine.

Free shadow-boxing

Thirdly, train the combinations by putting them into free shadow-boxing using slipping and other body evasion and evading footwork. Mix the combinations that you're drilling with single direct attacks. Shadow-boxing is an excellent way to build skill. You need imagination, but good shadow-boxing will internalise all your techniques and give you warrior skills without being hit. If you don't know what to do, just concentrate on one or two combinations and intersperse them with a jab or double jab, and use one or two simple ways of moving. To work at different ranges, use elbows and knees in the same format as the punches that you've learnt already. Relax and play with the timing and footwork. Once you have some sparring experience then you can bring this experience to bear to update your game. Shadow-boxing is a great way to build confidence and a 'can do' mentality in your head before going

14: Rhythm

To be combatively effective you have to have a simple plan which is also profound in its implications. When you are fighting you have no time for concepts and mind work; rather, the body must react based upon training routines and patterns, and improvise around intuition, sensitivity, body feel and intent. If you see all the various techniques as separate then this is a lot for your mind to work on and won't lead to functionality. Simplifying everything down to its core essence is the way to go.

Strikes can be performed in a variety of ways and from a variety of angles but when reduced down to their essence they tend to follow simple body patterns. Most multiple combinations are based around simple body rotation. Your choice of combinations of blows, such as uppercut and overhead or jab and cross, is guided by the angle that your body is at.

This means that the body's core is the essential region if you are changing punches, and the arms are just an addition, a way of taking the power generated at the core to the target. Hitting from the core of your body, you can change very quickly if you keep your blows tight. It also gives you the ability to change your intended blow late, so it's much harder for your opponent to counter.

The body rotation that you need to develop to effectively punch can be likened to a wheel being turned. A standard jab and cross would be like holding the wheel horizontally. Uppercut and overhand blows would be like holding the wheel at a forty-five degree angle on either side.

Multiple blows with the same hand, often done on the angle, still have to use the same body mechanics, except one beat of the double isn't delivered and instead is used to build the power to deliver the second blow.

Whether you are using punches or elbow strikes, the essential movement is the same. A good way to train your ability to put these together and to work your core is through practising rhythm drills.

Rhythm drills

Rhythm drills are carried out using the all of the punching methods we've covered plus the body evasion skills. This means that not only is your body learning how to move but you are learning timing. If you work through this chapter and seek to understand how to get rhythm and flow into your blows then you're well on your way to looking and, more importantly, hitting like a pro.

The beat pulse

In pop music, the beat pulse is the big beat on the drum that you tap your foot to. On a metronome (a timing pulse machine available from music shops) you'd set it to about 40-60 beats per minute, or one per second. Go slower if you need to, or choose a tune which you like and work out to this. It's important to see it as a dance and let it get into your body. Play with the pulse. If you miss it, just move until you find it. Losing it and finding it again are good for your sense of rhythm so don't get stressed about it. Enjoy moving.

First we see you first hitting two punches to a pulse. This is like flicking your hand out and catching a fly in the air. Next it's three or four punches to each pulse. Then do the three or four punches on the angle, then on the other side. Then, bob and weave once per pulse, then twice per pulse, then slip each way two to a pulse. Next, snapback twice to a pulse. Then mix any two. Uppercut very short, four or eight to the pulse, up and down in the middle. Now play all of these together. Once you own the beat you

Two punches to a pulse

Three or four punches to a pulse

Three or four punches on the angle

Bob and weave once per pulse

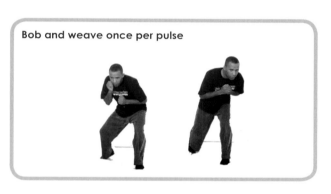

Slip two to a pulse

Snapback twice to a pulse

Mix any two

Uppercut very short

can play at losing the beat or striking just before or just after. It's like jazz: be discordant and then be in the beat. Both are valuable.

When I originally studied boxing, I initially learned to punch on the beat at an angle across my body – fast and light – much like trying to catch a fly. Once I had this then I would do it for two or three to the beat. Do this on the spot. Obviously, if you are going faster the blows have to be abbreviated, but your body is still working. Get your shoulders to be loose and moving. There should be a loose bouncy fluid feel when doing this. Then add this to simple evasion skills like slipping and bobbing and weaving, ducking and snapback. Do all of these on the beat or in relation to the beat. Then you have a sort of improvised dance which can focus on just one aspect, like the punching or the evasion, or mix it up into a type of shadow-boxing – but concentrating on rhythm.

Once you can do the rhythm drills on the spot then you can start to move around and use footwork, dropping in and out of the rhythm. Every now and again go back and go over the basics like slipping or bobbing and weaving. Because this type of training goes into your body through the route of music, it goes much deeper. Relax, let the rhythm take you and find your own way of dancing/fighting.

I remember seeing dancer Gene Kelly and boxer Sugar Ray Robinson tap dancing together and Robinson was by far the better mover. It showed when he fought.

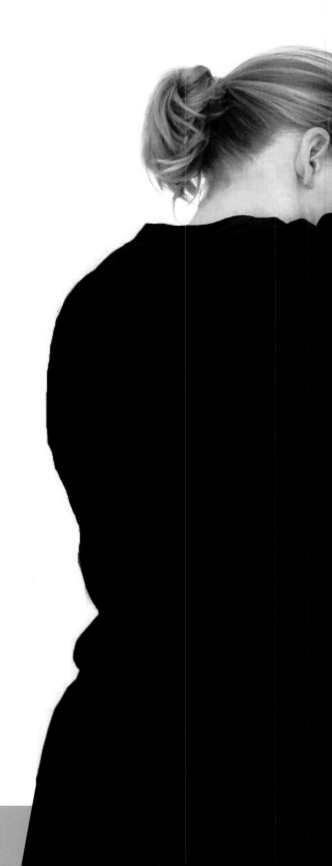

15: Timing

To help you to understand one aspect of timing and to emphasise the importance of being pro-active I'm going to explain the combat time line. This gives you a way to understand how you can change the nature of a move depending upon its position along the time line. Then you have a simple plan but lots of built-in variation.

At one end of the combat time line, you are fighting pro-actively; at the other, reactively. When you're fighting, you can do things before his attack, during his attack or after his attack. Stopping your opponent before he gets started is the best tactic as you limit his choices and take control of the situation. However, in the reality of combat you don't always get to choose the ground or time where you will have to attack or defend. Therefore you have to adapt. Understanding the time line gives you a better understanding of how things work, which should make you more adaptable. It should also make you realise that any technique works only so long as it's functional. The time line is just a tool which you can use to improve your training, so don't get too obsessed with it. If you're being successful then keep on doing what you are doing; if not then the time line may help, alongside further work to refine your technical skills.

Fighting time line

Once you are fighting there are a number of things which tend to happen all the time. These constants are what I will try to explain in this chapter. Once you've understood the time line you can see a simple game plan that you can apply in every fight.

1. Pre-empt

The first time line tactic is to strike your opponent before he gets started on attacking you, when he's just started to plan his attack. You see the intention, the gleam in his eye and attack before he does. This can be hard to explain legally, as a gleam in the eye can't be picked up on CCTV, or by witnesses if it's a street fight. If it's a sparring session then this is absolutely fine. Real fighting ability is based on being guided by your intuition. Not getting in the way is something that should be cherished when it happens.

2. Stop-hit

Secondly, you could attack on his preparation, the moment he starts to attack you. This is the aptly-named stop-hit or stop-kick we covered in Part 3. This is highly effective and is an essential part of your game. You hit him when he's just getting started. Most opponents telegraph their blows in some way or other. This is some sort of movement on his part that lets you know the attack is coming, if you know what to look for. Often it's just a matter of observing and noting the small routine things that he does when he attacks.

Telegraphing

Telegraphing is something that you should concentrate on eliminating from your own attacks. Often this isn't simply a raising of an elbow or clenching of a fist before the attack, or even a raising of the eyebrow. It can be something specific like this, but sometimes it is just that your opponent has a certain rhythm that he falls into when he is going to launch an attack, and he'll repeat this starting dance each time he commences fighting. You can attack on both specific telegraphic moves that he does and on his dance that leads to an attack. It's important to keep observing in all your training.

If you don't take this pre-emptive approach then you are into the interactive, trading type of combat that makes up most of fighting.

3. Evasion

Evasion and counter-punching are the next things to do in your hierarchy of tactics. What makes this most effective is good footwork and body movement.

Footwork

You can use footwork to stay at a suitable distance from your attackers' limbs, either just out of range or off his line of attack. You should try to be constantly moving so that his big guns can't get a good line on you whilst all of your own big attacks are there, at a distance, and pointing at your opponent.

Snapback

Secondly, you can stay at a medium-to-close distance and either snap in and out of range using snapback, or evade using slipping and body evasion.

Close-quarter counter-punch

If you are attacked with moves that penetrate deeper into your circle then you have a third option. Slip, or evade, and move into close range with your opponent doing most of the work to close the distance. By evading and counter-punching like this, you will find that you can hit really hard, as long as your structure is good. You don't have to be fast, though you do often have to show some courage to do the minimal amount of movement and stand your ground. Counter-punching like this is the most effective way of hitting hard. The way to train this is by doing lots of repetition and understanding the science and effectiveness of this approach. The

closer you are, the harder it is for your opponent to hit you and the more skilful your attacker needs to be. He has done all the work of covering the distance between you. This is now a job that you don't have to do; all you have to do is make sure that you are off the line of attack. Once you are here at close range you can strike, throw, or strike and then throw, or move to your opponent's back where he is in an inferior position.

4. Block & parry

Blocking or parrying is your fourth recourse. Normally, in training, these blocks and parries are practised so that you do them during or at the end of his attack. Often, however, this isn't the most effective way to use them. Like the striking, blocks and parries can be moved in both directions along the time line.

It's at middle range that the hand defence techniques that I've shown in this book are at their most useful and this is what much of your training is about. These can be done in three ways: before, during or after your opponent's action. One is to use the block or parry before his attack gets started. This is a very effective way of closing him down and is much like a stop-hit, but is a stop-parry or block. You use the block to trap him. Many trapping techniques can be used like this, before your opponent gets started. Often I will tell students that the two things to do at the start of their opponent's attack is first to strike him and second to imbalance him. Use the parry or block to do this. Play with his balance.

Doing blocks and parries during your opponent's attack is effective mainly if you are going to counter-punch. It's important not to stop his forward momentum but to redirect it. Make sure in your practice that you don't over-block as this can leave you vulnerable to trapping.

If you are not going to counter-attack then move,

don't block. The reason that you block or parry is to keep you at a range or position where you can deliver attacks. Even blocking can be dangerous, so why take chances if you aren't going to strike?

Lastly, you can sometimes block at the end of the attack and follow your opponent back. This can be done just to keep the line closed as you counter-attack, or to trap or jam him so that he can't defend as well.

Application of the time line

So how do you go about learning where and when to apply your time line tactics? The best way to build the stop-hit, or any other action, into your game is to use it all along the time line. That is, jab all the time or front kick all the time, whether it's as a stop-hit or after your opponent's attack. This will make you better at applying that technique, and you'll also learn the best times to use it. Pretty soon you'll find that you are stop-hitting much more often, but are not under time pressure and you'll realise that it can be used all along the time line.

Let me explain. Have one or two stop-hits like the jab or front kick that you focus on doing all the time. Then if you are successful and get your chosen attack in as your opponent attacks, it's a stop-hit. On the other hand, if it's a bit late then it's a simultaneous block or evade and hit. Bruce Lee termed the simultaneous block and hit 'Lin sil da'.

If you attack after, then you've either blocked and counter-attacked with a kick or punch, or you've counter-attacked after the attack has missed. Blows normally miss because the distance is too great or because the blow or strike is slightly curved; it then has what we call a closing line and an opening line. The closing line is the diminishing gap in front of his blow; the opening line is the increasing gap behind the blow. If possible, hit into the opening line.

The crush can be used almost anywhere on the time line. Use it early to jam, or as a shield which enables you to strike and enter behind, or just as a way to spike his attack.

Just adding the concept of 'before, during and after' to your training and sparring practice will make you a much better fighter. It's a simple plan, but hugely powerful.

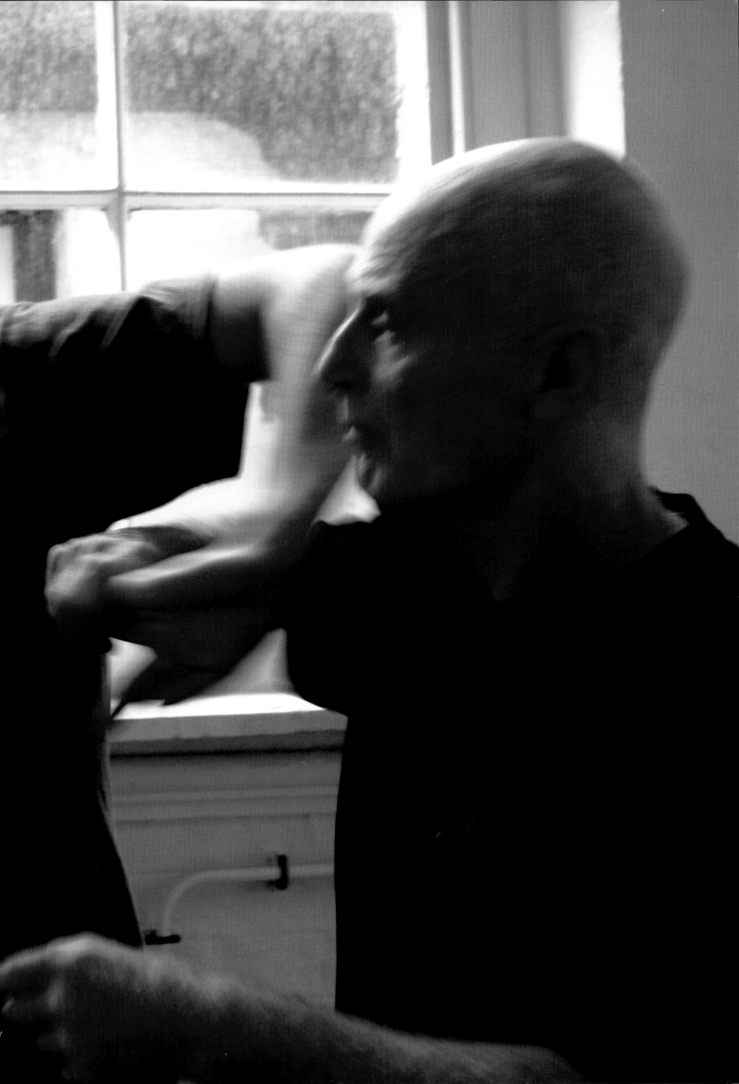

What happens when you hit them?

Fighting is complicated and there are no simple rules that guarantee success. However, understanding the basic format that fighting often falls into helps you in both your study and application.

In this chapter I'll show some common scenarios that happen in combat and ways to use the techniques covered in this book to deal with them.

If your opponent has been hit, either before he got started or by some defensive gambit on your part, he tends to do a number of things which you can prepare for and deal with more effectively when they happen. Even if you, or he, has missed, he may still do some or all of them.

Scenario 1: He retreats, you follow

If your opponent has been struck, he may retreat, and you can follow him back with kicks or the combinations which we have covered earlier. Don't over-reach, or chase a retreating opponent too hard. Work only where you are evenly balanced and don't get too greedy; people are often knocked out as a result of being too persistent in their counter-attacks. Think of your opponent as a spring. If you compress him too much, he will spring back at you. Judge the point at which you've got some advantage and then decide either to continue your attack until your opponent drops, or, if your intuition tells you that he may do one last desperate flurry, you can let him out to do a floundering counter-attack and then hit him again at the end of this. In fighting, this judgement is hard to get and is built on experience. Act like a pro and keep a cool head. You'll get further this way.

If you've hit your opponent effectively he may fall to the ground and the fight is effectively over. Be careful to make sure that he is totally down. In street fighting it's always best to use a finishing technique like a knee drop or round kick to a seated opponent to make sure he doesn't bounce back up whilst you deal with the next opponent.

Use your sparring in the dojo to get into good habits, including finishing your opponents, even if it's only shadow-boxing style in the air. Don't leave an active opponent on the floor. Another thing to work on is what the Japanese call 'Zanshin' (awareness) where you keep alert to the dropped opponent and treat him as a threat at all times. It's important to do this when doing training drills. Often people turn their back or don't pay attention at the end of drills and build in bad habits that will get them hurt in real fighting.

Scenario 2: He is stopped but re-groups and comes again

Sometimes an opponent is stopped by your blow but re-groups and then comes again. Here you get the chance to do all the former stuff again, or you can punish him for advancing by 'sticking and moving': jabbing him hard as he attempts to advance and then using footwork to keep out of trouble. Keep him on the end of this stiff jab until he loses heart. Sometimes you can let your opponent expend some energy with a floundering attack and then strike him again when he runs out of steam. As you can see in these examples, good footwork is essential.

Above all, don't panic. You are ahead and just need to keep your cool and repeat what you've already been successful doing.

Scenario 3: He advances

If an opponent crashes in towards you this normally occurs in one of two ways. One is more passive in nature. This is where you've hit him hard and his instinct is to get closer and smother your blows. Sometimes this is done with his head up but most often your opponent comes in with his head down or turned slightly from your attack, with his arms outstretched to make contact. The second is a more active style where your opponent wants to close and tackle or throw you. Nevertheless, you can treat both these ways as one, though you have to perform to a higher standard against a more active and aggressive opponent or a trained wrestler.

In the simplest example you can short knee your opponent to deny him the tackle, then chase him back or drop him with combinations of strikes. Alternatively, you can achieve some control over your opponent's body, for example with a head and arm control, and slam him into hard objects, take him down and do a ground finish. You can also divert your opponent's clinch or attack attempt much like a matador does to a bull.

Scenario 4: Clinch

Another scenario is when you fall into a clinch or tie up position after your blows. This is a huge area that warrants its own book. However, we have covered a number of the simple options here and this should give you a good place to start. From the clinch the fight could then go to grappling or throwing. You are better off having a small number of throwing techniques that you can master. In this book we have concentrated on some high percentage throws that are easy to do and that happen often. The head and arm throw is often a good place to start and can be adapted to be a pure hip throw if needed. The head is a huge target and you should have escapes from basic head controls as part of

your game. Think in all close quarter fighting about the four directions that you can move in, and train so that you have some sort of technical skill in all four directions. Above all, be active, not passive. When clinching, as in most things, it's essential to keep a good base so you are harder to move or throw. If possible, strike, as this denies many of the grapplers' advantages. Grappling is a much bigger area and beyond the scope of this book but you should make sure you have some knowledge of ground fighting as a fundamental part of your art.

In all fighting make sure you are the hammer and not the nail. Be active not passive and take the fight to him. Even if you are moving backwards, ensure that you have forwards intent. This will give you positive mental feedback and more confidence. Above all, be the hunter, not the hunted.

Conclusion

Fighting is complex but you can enhance your study of it by learning the fundamentals well and welding together a plan that will make you more successful. Once you've got this then you can add more complex and esoteric techniques to the mix. I see many students with lots of knowledge yet with no framework within which to work. The aim of this book has been to give you some of the keys to integrating your knowledge and to see where all the diverse approaches can be used as part of your game. I have, of course, focused on basic skills. You can adapt these to other tools, or use simpler combinations; it's the concept that's important and for this reason I haven't focused on the complexities of close-quarter work, trapping and locking. Within this book there are many techniques and concepts that, if you take the trouble and time to master, will make you into a truly formidable stand-up fighter.

There are a number of things you need to guarantee success. Most important is a good teacher or instructor. Be prepared to travel for the right input, though if you have an open and inquiring mind and a friendly disposition it's amazing how many incredible people live near you and from whom you can learn. A good instructor may not be of the style of fighting that you follow but great instructors are to be treasured when you find them, whatever system they teach. Realise that some of the best teachers may not be the most well-known. Judge a teacher by his students. Are they respectful, friendly and skilful? Tough, swaggering people are often found on the outside of the ring, telling those inside what they should be doing, whereas the ones inside tend to be a bit humbler and more in the real world. You'll be spending lots of time with these people, so choose well. You in turn have to be a good student. What does this mean? To me, it means a person who turns up and does his work, whose focus is on quality. As comedian Woody Allen said, '90% of being successful is just turning up.' A good student doesn't complain, but shows his interest by his actions, not his words. Over the years I've met numerous students who like to talk about how much training they are doing or fights they've had or masters they've learnt from. Then they move, and you can see instantly exactly what they've been doing and at what level they are. Don't waste your time talking when you could be training.

To be successful, you need to be consistent in your practice. This doesn't mean training every day; this will lead to over-training and injury. Three or four good sessions per week with a bit of other study from books or DVDs, plus conditioning training, is easily enough. You learn more when you rest; your body grows after the stimulus of training and your brain has the time to sort things out which it can't do when you are constantly training.

If you are going to be serious in your study it's important to have a support structure. This could include physical therapists who can help if you get injured and most importantly good training partners who share some of your goals. If you want a good support structure you have to be one to others. Give advice when needed, be supportive and keep them real. Martial arts is full of wild dreams and theories, lots of them based on hope. Keep a base in reality but be prepared to think the unorthodox.

Use this book as it's intended: as a base from which to work. Realise that you're more important than any style or system. Learn the rules and then break them; 'if it works, it's good' is the moral here. Research your own experience. Where do you end up all the time? Then research that position or area, become expert, and take it from there.

Martial arts is vast and will lead you on a voyage of discovery, not only on your own inwards journey learning about fear, trust, determination, diligence and self-discipline but also by awakening your senses. Through that it will lead you to an appreciation of different cultures, different rhythms and music, and hopefully a feeling of increasing peace – all from a fighting art. Good luck and good training.

Drills and work-ou

Triangle footwork

Triangle footwork is used a lot in Filipino and Indonesian martial arts where each point of the triangle could be the start of another triangle so that you have a huge range of ways of moving. This is mainly for dealing with multiple opponents. Here I've just done simple triangle steps to build leg strength and a double-sided approach to body development. Use these attributes for tackling or evading or as a challenging warm-up. Do rounds of two or three minutes or until your legs get tired.

> Forwards triangle. You can do this with a length of chain or a long stick like a Japanese Bo, dropping under the strike to make sure you drop low enough. Builds courage and entering skills

> Forwards triangle and punch. Punch to the stomach. Aim for the same target regardless of which leg is forward

> Forwards triangle and long knee

> Forwards triangle and jab and cross (different leads each side). Hit the same targets whichever leg is forward

> Forwards triangle and side kick to the knee or stomach

> Triangle away from round kick and cut kick to the standing leg

> Triangle away from the round kick and side kick to the knee

> Reverse triangle and spinning side kick to static opponent

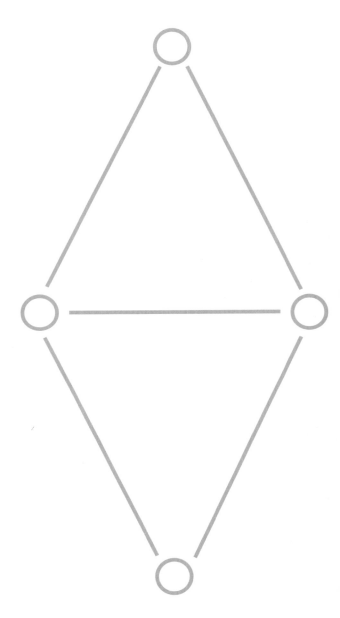

Crush drills with a partner

Do the following in sets of ten or until you've got them down. Then slowly mix together, working on keeping a central balance, raised hips and strong eyes focused on the opponent. Don't look at the kick, look at the opponent's chest.

1. Tree drill

Outside crush slowly, then inside crush for one to two minutes without putting the foot down. Think body structure; hips up, back strong. Builds balance, strength and proprioception.

2. Partner drills

Attacker	Defender
Jab – rear round kick	Parry – lead outside crush
Cross – lead round kick	Parry – lead cross crush
Jab – cross – lead round kick	Parry – parry – rear leg crush
Jab – rear round kick – lead round kick	Parry – lead leg outside crush – same leg cross crush
Jab – cross – lead round kick – rear round kick	Parry – parry – rear outside crush – same leg cross crush
Jab – cross – hook – rear round kick	Parry – parry – cover – crush
Then add counter kicks	
Jab – rear round kick	Parry – outside crush to same leg front kick
Jab – cross – lead round kick	Parry – parry – cross crush – lead front kick
Jab – cross – lead and rear round kick	Parry – parry – rear outside crush – cross crush – same leg front kick
Cross – lead round kick	Parry – crush either leg – rear round kick

This is just a sample way to work. Start by just isolating the crush and getting that right. Have it at the right angle and don't let it fold. Then go on to combination crushing with the same leg. Then use one leg after the other for combination kicks. It's not as simple combatively but your balance improves as you have to be central and not have the weight on one leg or the other. Once you've got that idea, follow up with a front kick without putting your foot down, to build core strength and ability. Then change the follow-up kick to a round kick as in the last couple of examples, or knee, hands or even plumm.

Knee workout

Do this with a partner. Put your hands on each other's shoulders, to keep the range only, not for support.

Long knee

Remember to turn the hip a little so the back doesn't take all the strain. It should go inwards, not upwards. Do one three-minute round using both legs equally.

Combinations

Do this on the Thai pads or, if you're with a partner, use the defences shown below.

Attacker	Defender
Jab – long knee	Parry – chest check
Jab – long knee	Parry – opposite hip check
Jab – cross – long knee	Parry – parry – chest check
Jab – cross – lead long knee	Parry – parry – opposite hip check
Jab – cross – lead long knee	Parry – parry – same side hip check
Jab – cross	Parry – double parry – long knee
Jab – cross	Parry – rear elbow crush / high cover – long knee
Jab	Rear parry – lead low round kick – middle rear round kick – lead knee

Power workout: Thai pads

In this very simple four-minute workout the emphasis isn't on doing the relevant techniques quickly, but, more importantly, making them heavy. Go at the pace that will allow you to put your body weight behind the blow or kick. Remember that you're just transferring bodyweight through your arms or legs; don't let it end in them. If you can feel it in the arms then it's in the arms. Let it go, feel empty and let the weight drop through.

Do each of the following for 30 seconds:

> Jab and cross

> Grab and knee

> Left round kick

> Right round kick

> Left and right horizontal elbows

> Front kick – round kick

> Lead front kick – round kick

> Finish with push-ups or plank or burpees

Punching workout

Static straight-blast punching

Slowly, one arm sliding over the other.

Moving side horse stance

Slowly, in a continuous manner.

Focus pads

Round one:

3 mins; Jab, double jab, jab – cross, and jab – cross – hook. Use your footwork. You can do them in any order, but a good place to start is by doing 20 of each or until you get a constant sound off the pads. Eventually, mix against a standard V hold or get your pad-holder to call the shots. Finish in the last half-minute with straight blast punches against pads.

Round two:

Three count punching, derived from the five count drills. Basically, do cross – hook – cross variations. Don't charge in too much; imagine you're with an opponent who refuses to back off and you're having a bit of a war. Move left and right or snapback between each combo. Last half a minute: straight blast.

Round three:

This round is focused on the bob and weave and the slip.

Single bob and weave against a hook. Come up and cross – hook – cross or variant.

Single bob and weave against a wide cross. Come up with hook – cross – hook or variant (double body or body – head hook – cross – hook – cross.

Double-bob and weave against double-left and right (or right and left) blows. Come up with either cross – hook – cross or hook – cross – hook-based combos.

Let the opponent's arm scrape the top of your head. Keep movement to a minimum. Use a combination of head movement and feet movement to bob and weave. Finish with half a minute straight blast on pads.

Round four:

Slip opponent's jab and rear uppercut – hook. Push opponent if he's too close and move right.

Slip opponent's quick jab with rear uppercut – lead uppercut – cross. Left hook – jab away and move right.

Slip opponent's straight right. Uppercut – cross – left hook and move away.

Slip opponent's straight right. Lead uppercut – rear uppercut – hook – cross – jab away – move right.

Slip opponent's straight right – lead uppercut – rear uppercut – cross (same hand) – left hook – move away to the right.

Finish with push-ups for 30 seconds.

Simple footwork and punching drills

Use these simple footwork patterns with basic punches so that you know that, under pressure, you'll have the right body position. It will mean that there's no dead time before you launch either an attack or counter-attack. I've used simple back and forwards motions first, then worked on simple sideways movements. Do the repetitions so that it gets into your bones, then use the footwork and associated strikes in sparring. 'If you use it it's yours, if you don't it's still mine!' Do each group or just one from each group for a three minute round.

Forwards and backwards

> Attack, stepping forwards, with jab – jab

> Step back (step and slide) two steps and jab – jab

> Attack, stepping forwards, with jab – jab

> Step back (step and slide) two steps – jab – cross

> Attack with jab – cross

> Step back (step and slide) two steps – jab – cross

> Attack with jab – cross

> Step back (step and slide) two steps and jab – jab

Combatively, moving straight back isn't that desirable. Two legs going forwards is faster than two going backwards. Once you've got the forwards and backwards idea, work on being less rigid in your lines and once you've gained distance ,move off his line of attack.

Never going back? I've coached lots of people who always concentrated on going forwards and who weren't interested in the idea of rearwards movement. Once they'd been in a real fight or competition and spent most of the time going backwards they worked the rearwards and curving footwork much more and were better fighters.

Sideways and curving

> Jab – cross. Move left (step and slide or shuffle/bounce) and jab – cross

> Repeat to the right

> Jab – move with L step to the right or around in a curve

> Jab – cross – move with L step and walk to the right or around in a curve. Re-insert lead leg – jab – cross

> Double jab – move with L step and walk to the right. Re-insert lead leg – jab – cross

> Once you've run out of space, shuffle back to the other end of your training space

> Jab – curve left – double jab – curve right – jab and cross – curve left – jab – cross – hook – curve right. And so on; you get the idea.

About the author

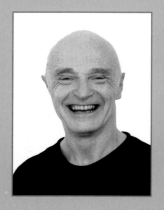

Probably one of the most unique individuals in the martial arts world, Bob Breen is renowned for his teaching abilities and his knowledge. He has captained his country in international competition in two differing martial arts and has been at the forefront of martial arts development throughout his career. To many, Bob is an inspiration; a period of health problems led him to have a double hip replacement and he continues to suffer from severe food allergies. However, he is still in training, fighting and having fun and leads a superb team of staff and Instructors.

Bob is renowned as a specialist in close-quarter fighting. He teaches a synthesis of empty hand, stick and knife work, using integrated principles for all three areas. He is regarded by many, including Dan Inosanto, as being superb at close-quarter and one of the world's knife defence experts.

Bob began martial arts training in 1966 and from early 1967 began studying Wado Ryu under Tatsuo Suzuki. He continued in Wado Karate for a number of years and passed his black belt in 1970, passing his second degree in 1972. He continued to study Karate and associated arts, moving to Japan in 1974 where he trained under a variety of Senior Masters.

Bob competed internationally in Karate on a number of occasions. He was captain of the Amateur Martial Arts Association (AMA) team which beat the Japanese in 1974 – a new thing then. Bob then moved into boxing and groundwork and was one of the pioneers of full contact in Europe, both fighting and promoting.

In 1978 he started Eskrima with Jay Dobrin and in 1979 hosted the first Dan Inosanto seminar in the UK. Since this inspirational look at Jeet Kune Do and Filipino martial arts, he has been a disciple of Guru Dan Inosanto, a student of JKD and Kali concepts, and their use in combat. He is qualified as a Full Instructor in JKD and Kali under Dan Inosanto.

Bob is regarded as the father of JKD and the Filipino martial arts in Europe. He was the founder member of the World Eskrima Kali Arnis Federation in 1987 and founder of the European Arnis Kali Eskrima Federation in 1992. He fought in the first World Championships in the Philippines in 1989, as well as being team coach. He continued as coach in 1992 with a very successful team.

What sets Bob apart is his reputation as a teacher, producing many of the top instructors in the UK today. In 2000 Bob founded Jeet Kune Do-Kali International, an organisation dedicated to expanding the high quality teaching of Jeet Kune Do and Kali throughout Europe.

Acknowledgements

Sincere thanks to the excellent models featured throughout this book:

Joe Kerr

Stephanie de Howes

Peter Newton

Austin Plunkett

Owen Ogbourne

Carl Greenidge

Judy Breen

Julian Gilmour

Stephanie, Peter, Carl, Joe and Owen are available
as private tutors and can be contacted via

Bob Breen Academy

16 Hoxton Square

London

N1 6NT

0207 729 5789

Index

Visit www.bobbreen.co.uk for up to date information

about the Bob Breen Academy, including seminars and

classes.